BASEBALL ENGLISH

Philip S. Riccobono, Ph.D.
Baseball Scout, English Lecturer

Copyright © 2021 by Philip S. Riccobono

All rights reserved. No part of this book may be reproduced or used in any manner without written permission of the copyright owner except for the use of quotations in a book review. For more information, address: sportsEnglish1@gmail.com

ISBN: 978-0-578-89104-0

FIRST EDITION

Sports English Press
www.sportsEnglish.org

BASEBALL ENGLISH

Philip S. Riccobono, Ph.D.
Baseball Scout, English Lecturer

Acknowledgements

The author and publisher express gratefulness to those who have granted permission to reproduce extracts and adaptations of copyrighted material. Reproduced by permission: John Fitzgerald, Playing for Peanuts LLC. Reproduced by permission: Interview with Shane Youman by Jeff Liebsch, Haps.

The author and publisher express gratefulness to those who have granted permission to reproduce extracts and adaptations of material written for this book. Reproduced by permission: Foreword by Don Nomura. Reproduced by permission: Interview with Joe Furukawa. Reproduced by permission: Interview with Conor Brooks. Reproduced by permission: Interview with Jessica Neitz. Reproduced by permission: Interview with Manabu Kuramochi. Reproduced by permission: Interview with Noboru Katsuragawa. Reproduced by permission: Interview with Chaewoo Lim. Reproduced by permission: Interview with Jeeho Yoo. Reproduced by permission: Interview with David Kim. Reproduced by permission: Interview with Brandon Knight. Reproduced by permission: Interview with Mike "Nino" Ninivaggi. Reproduced by permission: Interview with Taka Sakurai. Reproduced by permission: Interview with Steve Cohen. Reproduced by permission: Interview with Shane Youman by Jeff Liebsch, Haps Magazine. Reproduced by permission: Creative Commons batting stance.

The author and publisher would like to thank the following for their kind permission to reproduce photographs and other visual aids. Unit 1: John Fitzgerald (inside dugout), Merry Steward/pixy.org (home plate), John Fitzgerald (clubhouse), John Fitzgerald (tarp), Ray Shrewsberry/pixabay.com (scoreboard), Nicole De Khors/Burst (base), Creative Commons (warning track), Sam Smith (foul pole), John Fitzgerald (coaches, umpires meet), John Fitzgerald (kitchen), Joe Furukawa (media conference), Joe Furukawa (on-field with Marty Brown). Unit 2: Jack Kasarjian/xbats.com (specialized bat), John Fitzgerald (coach and player), John Fitzgerald (coach giving sign), PXhere.com (player bunting), John Fitzgerald (Wally Backman smiling), Adam Klepsteen/Freeimages.com (players), John Fitzgerald (clubhouse meeting), John Fitzgerald (Mike Colacchio smiling), John Fitzgerald (mound conference), Conor Brooks (BP coach side angle), Conor Brooks (BP coach throws). Unit 3: Keith Johnston/Pixabay.com (umpire punchout), chrisoleary.com (arm slot), Unsplash.com (baseball seams), Paul Brennan (pitcher's mound), DanBlewett.com (rubber), Keith Johnston/Pixabay.com (umpire calls strike), TopVelocity.net (players on-field), PXhere.com (pitcher), DanBlewitt.com (pitching grip), PXhere.com (center field view of home plate), PXhere.com (first baseman and runner), chrisoleary.com (inverted W), Dr. Rafael Escamilla (arm angles), Probaseballinsider.com (pitching grip), DanBlewett.com (pitching grip), Creative Commons (pitching grip), Creative Commons (pitching grip), Creative Commons (pitching grip), DanBlewett.com (curveball), DanBlewett.com (slider), DanBlewett.com (knuckle curve), DanBlewett.com (changeup), Chris Nowlin/Knuckleballnation.com (pitching grip), Creative Commons (pitching grip), John Fitzgerald (mound conference), John Fitzgerald (Wally Backman talks with pitcher), Jeff Liebsch/Haps (Shane Youman throwing), Shane Youman (t-shirt front and back). Unit 4: Pexels.com (fielder and runner at second base), Jannis Paulk/freeimages.com (youth player), Matt Antonelli/AntonelliBaseball.com (players running), Doug Bernier/ProBaseballInsider.com (close-up of player's glove), PXhere.com (player in outfield), Matt Antonelli/AntonelliBaseball.com (bending), Diamond Sports (special equipment), John Fitzgerald (infielders talk), John Fitzgerald (autographed team photo, players chat with fan, player and fan shake hands), Jessica Neitz (two Cambodian baseball members with national flag, Cambodia Men's National Team). Unit 5: PXhere.com (player at bat), Doug Sharp/Newton Athletic Club (coach and hitter), Stick & Ball TV, gameSense Sports Channel (hitting practice), Creative Commons (youth player swings), Creative Commons (hitter indoors), Doug Bernier/ProBaseballInsider.com (player on basepath), John Fitzgerald (runner on third base), Creative Commons (hitting equipment indoor), Creative Commons (hitter illustration), PXhere.com (youth fielder and runner), Dr. David Kagan (baseball directions), Library of Congress (Highlanders at Hilltop Park), John Fitzgerald (Wally Backman), Dave Hogg/Creative Commons (McGwire bat), Creative Commons (batting stances), John Fitzgerald (Wally Backman and Cecil Fielder), John Fitzgerald (view from behind backstop), John Fitzgerald (player and coach celebrate), John Fitzgerald (play at the plate). Unit 6: PXhere.com (infielder), Chris Chow/Unsplash.com (hitter AB), Haley Hamilton/Unsplash.com (youth pitcher), Jose Francisco Morales/Unsplash.com (pitcher), Creative Commons (stopwatch), Sal Agostinelli (team executive and player), Keith Johnston/Unsplash.com (pitcher), Chris Nelson/Creative Commons (scouts), John Fitzgerald (Wally Backman reports), Doug Bernier/ProBaseballInsider.com (Doug Bernier, radar guns). Unit 7: The Billings Gazette (clubhouse), Creative Commons/Timothy Parish, USMC (two players and umpire), Tim Parsons/TahoeOnStage.com (team executive in office), John Fitzgerald (team personnel and players), Dr. Alan Nathan (donut hole), Creative Commons/USMC (Petco Park), The Billings Gazette (clubhouse), Joe Furukawa (interpreter and Yu Darvish), John Fitzgerald (manager and front office representative), John Fitzgerald (player, trainer, manager on-field), Noboru Katsuragawa (interpreter and player), Chaewoo Lim (at stadium), Jeeho Yoo (in stands), David Kim (jacket and baseball in hand), Mike Ninivaggi (mound conference), Taka Sakurai (trainer attends to injured player), Fred Claire (Claire and Nomo), CIFF/Creative Commons (Hideo Nomo), UCinternational/Creative Commons (Chan-ho Park). Unit 8: John Fitzgerald (manager and player, players speaking with manager), John Fitzgerald (break it up), Creative Commons/Library of Congress (song sheet).

The author and publisher would like to thank the following for their help and support in developing the book: Dr. Kiwan Sung, *Kyung Hee University*; Dr. William Eggington, *Brigham Young University*; Dr. Michele Lee, *Kyung Hee University*; Dr. Han-gyu Lee, *Kyung Hee University*; Dr. Shin-chul Hong, *Busan University of Foreign Studies*; Dr. Mark Davies, *Brigham Young University*; Dr. Marieta Simeonova-Pissarro, *University of Nevada Las Vegas*; Sal Agostinelli, *Philadelphia Phillies*; Michael Ninivaggi, *Wantagh High School Baseball*; Steven E. Quasha, *Sugiyama Jogakuen University*; Michael Kealey, *Yonsei University*; David Kim, *Minnesota Twins*; Jordan Eaves; Steve Horn, *Fox Sports*; Glenn Brown, *Kobe College*; Jonathan Lieb, *Kobe University*, Michael Parrish, *Kwansei Gakuin University*; Dr. Michael Greisamer, *Kobe City University of Foreign Studies*; Thomas St. John, *Sungkyunkwan University*; Josh Sullivan, *Georgia State University*; Troy Miller, *Aichi Bunkyo University*; James Ahn, *Doosan Bears*; David Zwillick; Paul Tanner, *Shiga University*; Steven Feigenbaum, *Sungshin Women's University*; "Cousin" Rudy Hinnant, *Nagoya Institute of Technology*; Jerry Halvorsen, *Hokusei Gakuen University*; Charles Barbato.

About the book

UNIT 1: Inside the park: On and off the field overview — 8
Parts of the ballpark and field, Value of learning about data, Rainouts, Indy ball players' home, Interpreter-mediator profile

UNIT 2: Go get 'em: What coaches have to say — 16
Manager, Coaches, Manager tirade, Hot dogs in the dugout, Kangaroo Court, Insider Advice from former MLB pitcher, BP coach profile

UNIT 3: Pitching: A large percent of the game — 26
Specialized vocabulary, Inverted W, Grips, Off-speed challenge, Controversial remarks

UNIT 4: Out in the field — 37
Infield, Outfield, "I got it!", Meet-and-greet, Woman saving lives and coaching in Cambodia profile

UNIT 5: Hitter-runner: Batter up! — 50
Hitting, Running, Too much spin, The sweet spot, Slump, Bunt, Tag up, Bunting: A lost art?

UNIT 6: Scouting — 62
Describing and evaluating players, Scout's job, Skills for each position, Scouting reports, Sal Agostinelli's important questions, Choosing a speed gun, International scouting director profile

UNIT 7: Now hiring: The many jobs in baseball — 75
Baseball jobs, Job skills, Interpret challenge, Front office calls, Why don't you…, Ups and downs of working in baseball, Finding the right job in baseball, Pioneer GM profile

UNIT 8: Baseballisms: A very unique, complex language — 92
Understanding baseball talk, Crossword challenge, Translation, Research in baseball vocabulary, Baseball podcasts, Red ass, International baseball expert, BONUS ACTIVITY: Learn baseball through song

About the book

Baseball English has been created specifically for people working, or preparing to work, in the baseball industry who often need to use English to communicate. Of course, this book may also serve baseball enthusiasts who want an insider's view of English for Baseball. The book will provide learners with the necessary vocabulary and language skills to understand normal situations in a baseball context and some settings in general English.

The book has eight units. The author used rigorous statistical testing with input from experts in the field of baseball to identify, for this book, corpus-driven vocabulary that is most frequently used and relevant in the sport. The book covers key positions on and off the field, from pitcher to general manager to the team clubbie. Units from the book work independently and can be selected according to the needs and interests of learners. *Baseball English* may be used for self-study.

Each unit begins with **Batter Up**, which includes corpus-driven vocabulary exercises and serves as an introduction to each unit topic. Practical exercises, video and listening extracts, industry-specific texts, and photographs, illustrations, and other visuals help you to acquire key vocabulary and expressions. Exercises such as role-playing, writing scouting reports, and finding a job in baseball offer learners chances to use practical sport-related language.

Units contain **Watch and Listen-In** videos consisting of **Insider Talk and Everyday English** from unscripted, authentic dialogue used in baseball from the TV documentary series, *Playing for Peanuts*. The videos center around vocabulary, listening, comprehension checks, discussion questions, and role-playing activities. Each unit ends with a **Reading Spotlight**, which includes profiles of people in baseball and other sport-related topics. Comprehension checks and discussion questions follow each reading. For convenience, you will find all video and audio extracts online.

The online appendix of *Baseball English* includes corpus-driven **A-Z Words and Phrases List** consisting of vocabulary frequently used and relevant in the sport. The list also includes new keywords and phrases that do not appear in the units of *Baseball English*. You will also find the **Answer Key** to all exercises so that you can check your answers if you are working alone. This will be especially valuable if you use *Baseball English* for self-study.

For all video and audio clips related to this book:
www.sportsEnglish.org/media

WARNING
May contain offensive language

Foreword

Baseball is a part of the sports, business, and entertainment worlds. It's a pastime that is fun, dramatic, and exciting, and it truly unites people around the world. From 1995 to today, many Asian players have crossed the Pacific to play in Major League Baseball. The business of baseball has found a totally new market to increase attendance, craft new products, and venture into many different aspects of this historic game.

With the age of the Internet and vast information, our society must adjust and understand different cultures and languages. The game has integrated people from different societies, cultures, and countries into one form of sports. It's phenomenal! As the years go by, the game will make necessary changes and adjustments to fit evolving needs and maintain its excitement for generations to come. With more people understanding the depth, toughness, and unity that this game offers, a wider range of communication will be created, as will a true enjoyment of baseball.

Don Nomura, Official MLBPA Certified Agent
Amuse Sports USA
Twitter: @donnomura

UNIT 1

Inside The Park

Topics: Parts of the ballpark, Rainouts, Indy ball players' home, The interpreter

1. Batter Up! Vocabulary

A. Guess the Meaning of Each Photo Below

B. Talkin' Photos
Discuss the photos
Try speaking in complete sentences

A

B

Work alone
single

OR

With a partner or group
double play, tirple play

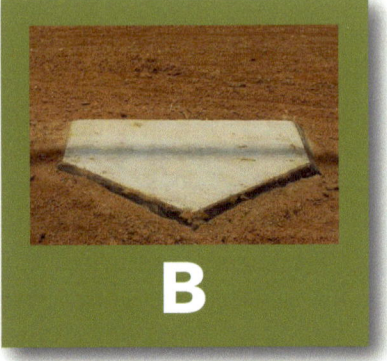
C

D

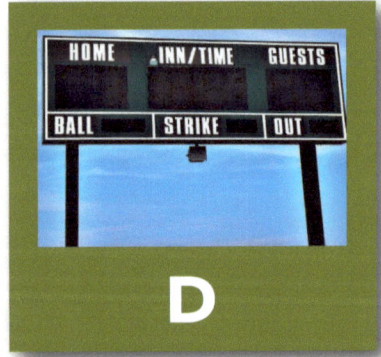
E

F

G

H

C. Match Each Photo With a Vocabulary Term

1. clubhouse/locker room
2. home plate/dish
3. warning track
4. dugout/bench
5. base/bag
6. foul pole
7. tarp
8. scoreboard

8

Vocabulary

A. Collocation Match-Up:
Match the two parts of these phrases.

1. _____ room   a. major
2. _____ league   b. bench
3. _____ track   c. game
4. _____ day   d. weight
5. _____ player   e. warning
6. _____ leagues   f. big

Did You Know?

Modern front offices value data, including advanced metrics/analytics, using it to find competitive ways to win. It helps to understand how to properly use this data. If you feel confident using it, you may have the skills to land a job in baseball, maybe even the front office. One way to start learning about working with such data is as a fantasy baseball league team owner. In Unit 7, you'll learn more about the front office and data in baseball.

1. Where can you find in-depth baseball data?
2. Why can working as a fantasy manager lead to a paying job in baseball?

B. Cluster Challenge:
Complete the collocations using these words:
locker/inning/field/game/bag/track

1. Baseball is a _____ of failure, right?
2. Yesterday we had another extra _____ game.
3. They aren't putting the tarp on the _____ .
4. The _____ room is right next door.
5. Did the ball make it to the warning _____ ?
6. I thought he beat him to the _____ .

C. Skill Practice:
Complete each sentence using the given vocabulary terms below.

1. He's one of the best players in the _____ , and he will probably continue to get better.
   a. minute b. game c. team
2. Dude, you're the best _____ in the world. You're the man!
   a. glove b. field c. clubbie
3. Foul pole to _____ all the way around on a fly is a home run.
   a. foul pole b. warning track c. dugout
4. Umpire: ground rules, the _____ is a home run.
   a. bag b. clubhouse c. scoreboard
5. How many people in this _____ think that they're going to the major leagues?
   a. locker room b. base c. scoreboard

2. Insider Baseball Talk: Bang it!

Let's go on the field and listen to an important conversation about the game between the managers, umpires, and a coach.

A. Watch and Listen-In (Video 1)
Please go to
www.sportsEnglish.org/media
Optional: Focus on watching the video at least one time before completing the gap-filling exercise below.

B. Gap-Filling:
Watch the video and fill in the blanks with the vocabulary you hear.

> **Wally Backman:** What are we doing?
> **Player:** He's about to call it. I said, he's about to call it right now.
> **Wally:** We better get the _____ on.
> **Wally:** Buddy, we're gonna need a tarp _____ .
> **Wally:** Tell me how _____ it is out there, _____ .
> **Wally:** Hey, if it _____ hard, we'll _____ .
> We'll play it _____ if we have to.
> **Umpire:** _____ just bang it.
> **Wally:** _____ _____ with you.

C. Pair Work
Grammar point: Banged = past tense of *bang*.
1. Research and discuss any unfamiliar vocabulary from the video.
2. Practice the conversation with a partner.

D. Discussion Questions
1. What does *bang it* mean?
2. Will they have a game tonight? Why or why not?
3. Who decides if the game is *banged*?
4. Why do baseball games get *banged*?

To watch more videos like this from *Playing for Peanuts*, go to Amazon Prime or Vimeo.

E. Conversation Strategy/Role Play

Notice that Wally uses *we* when asking for help and also when deciding whether to bang it.

Using *we're* makes his staff feel that they are all in this together as a team. Also, when he is speaking to the other team manager about banging the game, using *we* could make others feel like part of the decision-making process. So, remember that using *we* may help you gain cooperation from others.

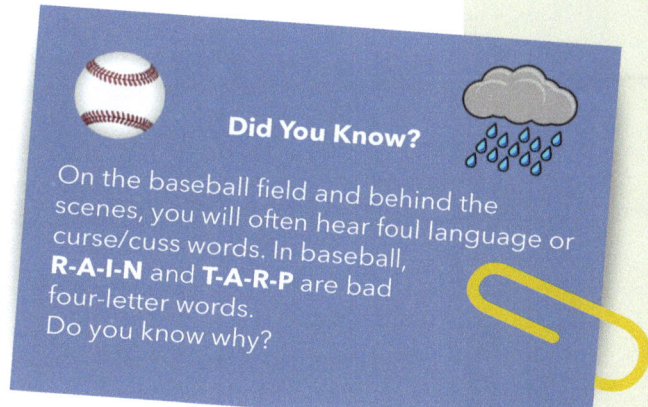

Did You Know?
On the baseball field and behind the scenes, you will often hear foul language or curse/cuss words. In baseball, **R-A-I-N** and **T-A-R-P** are bad four-letter words. Do you know why?

1. Try using *we or we are/we're* as a leader like Wally did when requesting a tarp pull.

2. Like Wally, try using *we* to make others feel like part of the decision-making process.

3. Reading: Baseball Trivia

Read. Are the Sentences True (T) or False (F)?
If False, make the statement True.

	True or False
ex. Sadaharu Oh hit more home runs than any player in pro baseball history.	T
1. The top North American baseball league is called Major League Baseball (MLB).	
2. Cuban National players (living in Cuba) can play in any league outside of their own.	
3. Players can leave a game and return to it at any time.	
4. Meiji Jingu Stadium is the oldest professional baseball stadium in Japan.	
5. Bases are spaced 75 feet apart in pro baseball.	
6. Masanori Murakami was the first Japanese-born player in MLB history.	
7. The Hanwha Eagles are based in Daejeon, South Korea.	
8. Chan-ho Park was the first Korean-born player in MLB history.	
9. Ozzie Virgil Sr. was the first Dominican-born player to play in MLB.	
10. MLB games can finish in a tie after 12 innings of play.	
11. Chen Chin-feng was the first Taiwan-born MLB player (in 2002 for the LA Dodgers).	

4. Everyday English: This is Fred.

Let's visit independent league baseball players and see how they live.

A. Photo Warm-Up
1. Discuss the photo below.
   Try to speak in complete sentences.
2. What do you think Steve is pointing to?
3. Where do you think Steve is?

B. General English Vocabulary
Match the italicized term with its meaning.

1. ___ bum		a.	bad or unfair deal
2. ___ broom		b.	living quarters
3. ___ dishes		c.	defends against others
4. ___ protects		d.	used to sweep the floor
5. ___ shafted (sl.)		e.	a small insect
6. ___ bug		f.	lazy person (used jokingly)
7. ___ trash		g.	garbage or waste
8. ___ refrigerator		h.	for serving food
9. ___ room		i.	chills food

C. Watch and Listen-In (Video 2)
Please go to www.sportsEnglish.org/media

Optional: Focus on watching the video at least one time before completing the gap-filling exercise below.

D. Gap-Filling:
Watch the video and fill in the blanks with the vocabulary you hear.

Steve: Alright let me show you the kitchen. This is the kitchen. You know, you got _____ in the corner and we haven't done dishes.
Steve: You know you got _____ in the corner and we haven't done dishes.
Steve: This is Fred. He protects our kitchen. It's a little _____ .
Steve: Here's our _____ .
Steve: Here's our refrigerator and our _____ .
Not a whole lot in there.
Steve: This is Dustin Taylor and Mike Colacchio's _____ . He's in bed right now 'cause he's the starting pitcher. He's a _____ !
Dustin: Getting a little rest.
Steve: They have the smallest _____ in the whole house. So, they kind of got _____ , as you can tell.

E. Practice
Read aloud the description of the player's home (D. Gap-Filling) with a partner.

F. Discussion Questions
1. Do you want to live in the house? Why or why not?
2. Why did Steve feel as though Dustin and Mike got shafted?
3. What do you like and dislike about this home?
4. Why do you think the guys live in this home?

G. Conversation Strategies

> When introducing people, places, or items, we can say, *This is*,
> ex. *This is* Fred. *This is* Dustin and Mike's room.
> To introduce a person, place, or thing, you can also use *Here is* or *Here's*,
> ex. *Here's* our broom.

Try It
Try using *this is* and *here is* with a partner.
ex. This is a pencil.
ex. Here's Joe.
This is…
Here is/Here's…

5. Reading Spotlight
Joe Furukawa: *Interpreter and Part Mediator*

A. Photo Warm-Up
1. What do you think the man on the right is doing? How about the man on the left?
2. What do you think the men's jobs are?

B. Vocabulary
Match the words that have similar meanings.

1. ___ interpreter   a. go-between
2. ___ interview   b. communicating
3. ___ language   c. conversation
4. ___ scout   d. evaluator
5. ___ mediator   e. well
6. ___ emotion   f. explainer
7. ___ um   g. feeling

C. Read

Optional: Try reading aloud with a partner. Take turns reading after a sentence or two.

Joe Explains

A familiar face around the Japan baseball scene is Joe Furukawa, Senior MLB Scout for the Texas Rangers. He is the former interpreter for All-Star MLB pitcher, Yu Darvish and former Hiroshima Carp manager, Marty Brown. Growing up in California, USA, Furukawa played high school and university baseball. He also played in Japan's top league: Nippon Professional Baseball (NPB). Furukawa worked with Yu Darvish in 2012 when he first came to the Texas Rangers. Darvish tried to speak English often: from introducing himself to new teammates to speaking to the media, Darvish wanted to improve. Often, he learned general and Baseball English from Furukawa. Darvish even told Furukawa that he had a goal of speaking in a press conference or interview using only English. Later in his MLB career, Darvish spoke to reporters in English. Darvish sent Furukawa a video clip of this and asked for his opinion on his English used in the post-game interview. Furukawa told him that his English progressed but still needed some improvement. Specifically, Darvish needed to try to eliminate saying, *"you know…you know"* so much.

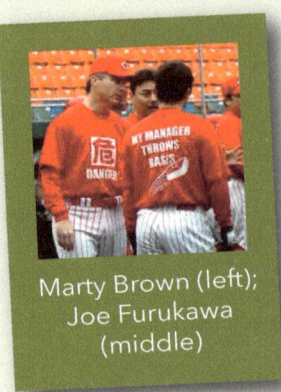

Marty Brown (left); Joe Furukawa (middle)

A few months later, the star Japanese player sent a video of a different interview for Furukawa to check. Furukawa felt that Darvish improved, hardly saying *you know*. Darvish valued his interpreter's opinion and worked to advance his English language ability, reaching a personal goal.

As an interpreter, Furukawa thinks that working this particular job in baseball is like being a mediator. He said, "You should not hold back, but ask the person if you really want me to say that." The reason for this is that it might cause a problem or misunderstanding. However, Furukawa also stresses the importance of interpreting with the same emotion as the person you interpret for; this sometimes includes foul language. Furukawa did this especially for Marty Brown, who was famous for using a lot of emotion sometimes when speaking to umpires. One time he got so excited that he even threw a base. This event was remembered on a funny team t-shirt—photo above.

The role of the interpreter in baseball is very important. The job not only entails conveying messages with meaning, but could also include other tasks such as language teaching and making sure players (and sometimes their families) are comfortable off the field all season long. It does help if you have a background in baseball.

D. Are the Sentences True (T) or False (F)?

1. Furukawa pitched for the Texas Rangers.
2. Yu Darvish tried to improve his language skills and eventually spoke to reporters in English.
3. Using *you know* too often when speaking English is something to avoid.
4. Having knowledge of Baseball English is advisable for future interpreters.
5. After asking the player or coach for permission to interpret everything said, interpreters must convey the message accurately and should not leave out anything said, using the same emotion.
6. Usually, interpreters have plenty of time off during the season and show up at the ballpark just before the first pitch.

E. Discussion Questions

1. Before scouting, what job did Joe Furukawa have?
2. Would you want to do Furukawa's job? Why or why not?
3. Why do you think Furukawa interpreted Japanese and English with emotion?
4. Do you think interpreters are necessary in baseball? Why or why not?

Go Get 'Em!

Topics: Manager, Coaches, Clubhouse talks, In-game discussion, Kangaroo Court, Insider Advice, Bullpen, Pitching coach

1. Batter Up! Vocabulary

A. Guess the Meaning of Each Photo Below

B. Talkin' Photos
Discuss the photos
Try speaking in complete sentences

Work alone
single

OR

With a partner or group
double play, triple play

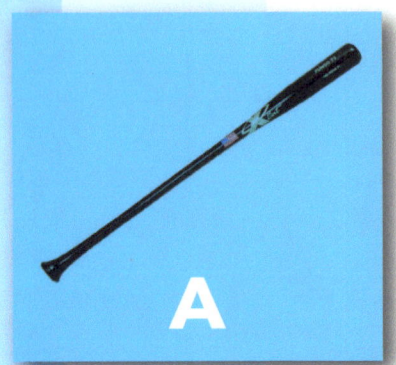
A

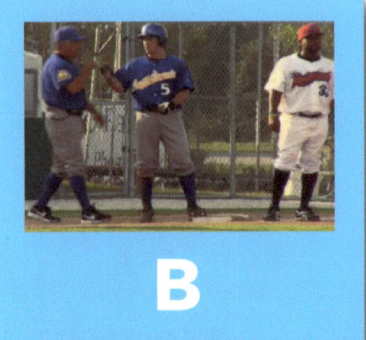
B

C

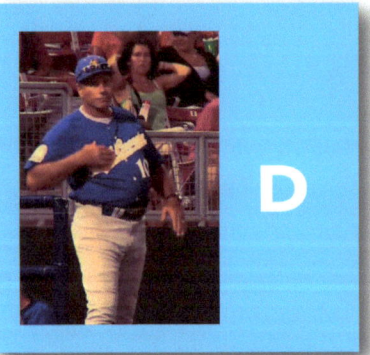
D

E

F

G

C. Match Each Photo With a Vocabulary Term
1. attaboy/that a baby
2. manager
3. fungo
4. bunt
5. lineup
6. bench players
7. sign

16

2. Vocabulary

A. Collocation Match-Up:
Match the two parts of these phrases.

1. ____ go   a. bunt
2. ____ staff   b. instructional
3. ____ coach   c. conditioning
4. ____ situation   d. coaching
5. ____ league   e. warning

B. Cluster Challenge:
Complete the collocations using these words:
college/pro/baseball/great/game

1. Baseball is a _____ of failure, right?
2. There you go, oh man, _____ play, Connor!
3. I'm Tommy, _____ instructor, and we're going to be talking about stretching exercises for baseball.
4. I picked this up from my _____ coach, John Smith.
5. I got a pro with me here. We've got Frank Mendez, who played eight years _____ ball: Boston, Minnesota, Cincinnati, and Seattle.

C. Skill Practice:
Complete each sentence said by managers or coaches, using the given vocabulary terms below.

1. Most of the places you go, you get fined for missing _____ I don't want your money, guys.
   a. hits b. signs c. strikes
2. My season was done; I went to _____ to rehab my torn rotator cuff.
   a. surgery b. instructional league c. the big league
3. Go, go! _____ Pete! Way to run the bases. That a baby!
   a. attaboy b. coach c. terrible
4. So the game starts now. When you are in the outfield shagging, you don't have to be gung-ho about it, but be professional about it and get the job done. Stay out of the outfielder's way and do things right. That's what puts your mind into a _____ mode.
   a. practice b. camp c. game
5. It's necessary for a pitching coach, a good one, to be a good buffer between the _____ and the pitchers.
   a. front office b. players c. manager
6. _____ Chris, big one right here, big one. Two out. Hey, two out!
   a. attaboy b. let's go c. stop

2. Insider Baseball Talk: Bang it!

Do the little things. Let's go inside the clubhouse and hear manager Wally Backman talk to his team after a game.

Warm-Up
Look at the photo below. What do you think the mood is in the clubhouse? Why?

A. Watch and Listen-In (Video 3)
Please go to www.sportsEnglish.org/media

Note: As mentioned before in this book, language used in baseball sometimes contains foul language or expletives. These expletives have been bleeped out of videos in this book. You may hear these videos unedited at www.sportsEnglish.org/uncut

Optional: Focus on watching the video at least one time before completing the gap-filling exercise below.

B. Gap-Filling:
Watch the video and fill in the blanks with the vocabulary you hear.

> **Wally:** Number one guys, that _____ *!!@*! my *!!@*!. They're *!!@*!. We were *!!@*!. We are not a _____ _____ hitting *!!@*! _____ _____ . We have to do the **little things** to _____ the games. We _____ _____, we _____ and _____ , we _____ . So, we got to do the little things and make it *!!@*! happen. You should be embarrassed _____ to them *!!@*!, I'll tell you that right now. I know we're **6 and 1** but we _____ like *!!@*!. So just get your *!!@*! together tomorrow, go out, take it out on them *!!@*!, they are not good. You guys are a lot better than that. We need guys out there to sign _____ , so go get 'em tomorrow.

"*!!@*! = expletive – An expletive is a word or phrase (such as "Damn it!") that people sometimes say when they are angry or in pain. It can be offensive or foul language."

C. Pair Work
1. Discuss any unfamiliar vocabulary.
2. Practice Wally's speech with a partner, taking turns each sentence or two. Try to use the same emotion as the manager.
3. What words could you replace with expletives that are not considered foul language? ex. *So just get your **act** together*.

D. Discussion Questions
1. What are the *little things*?
2. Why does the manager shout and use so many expletives in his speech?
3. What does *6 and 1* mean?
4. What does *take it out on them* mean?

Speaking Point: *Expletives*

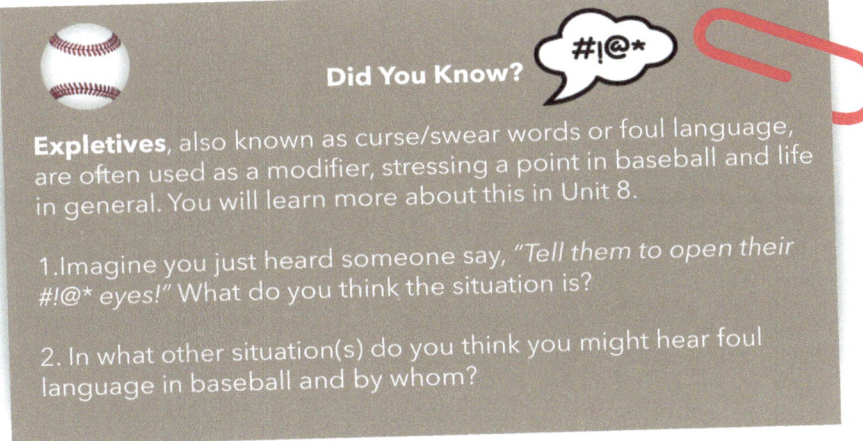

3. Everyday English:
How much did that hot dog cost you?
Rain delays might seem long and boring, but they can also be fun times.

A. Photo Warm-Up
Please answer in complete sentences.
1. What is one thing you see in this photo?
2. What is the player on the right about to eat?
3. Is there anything unusual about this photo? Please explain.
4. What's a rain delay?

B. Watch and Listen-In (Video 4)
Please go to
www.sportsEnglish.org/media
Let's go into the South Georgia Peanuts dugout for a conversation between manager Wally Backman and pitcher Mike Colacchio during a rain delay.

Optional: Focus on watching the video at least one time before completing the gap-filling exercise.

C. Gap-Filling:
Watch the video and fill in the blanks with the vocabulary you hear.

Wally: _____, you're not supposed to go up to _____ after 6. How much did that _____ _____ cost you?
Mike Colacchio: A _____.
Wally: Add $25 _____ to it.
Wally: I'll tell you what, if you go up and get 25 hot dogs, I, I won't _____ you the 25.
Player: Then I'll get fined again for going up there. So, it'll be 50.
Wally: You're right.

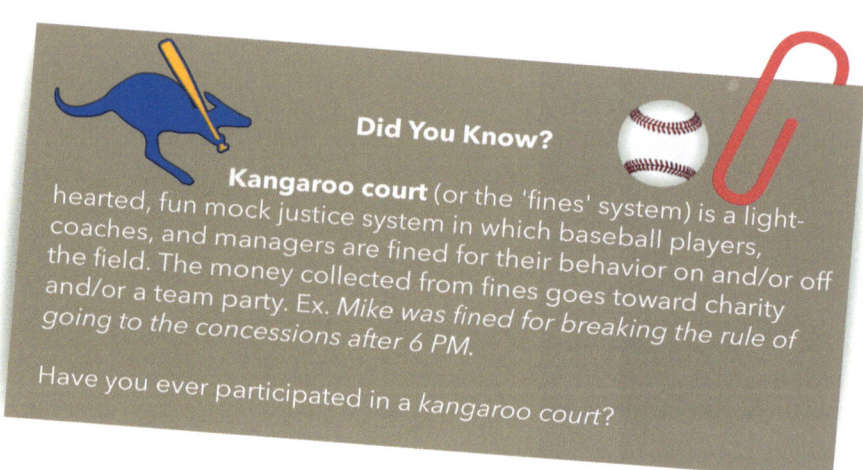

Did You Know?

Kangaroo court (or the 'fines' system) is a light-hearted, fun mock justice system in which baseball players, coaches, and managers are fined for their behavior on and/or off the field. The money collected from fines goes toward charity and/or a team party. Ex. *Mike was fined for breaking the rule of going to the concessions after 6 PM.*

Have you ever participated in a *kangaroo court*?

D. General English Vocabulary
Match the italicized term with its meaning.

1. ____ hot dog   a) money paid for breaking a rule
2. ____ concessions   b) dollars
3. ____ bucks (sl.)   c) sausage served on a long, sliced bun
4. ____ a dollar   d) unit of currency
5. ____ fine   e) informal way to get one's attention
6. ____ Hey   f) small shops in the ballpark

E. Discussion Questions
1. Why did Wally add $25 US onto what Mike paid for the hot dog?
2. If you were the manager, would you fine a player for going to buy a hot dog during a rain delay? Why or why not?
3. What do you think Wally wanted to use 25 hot dogs for?
4. What are typical foods and other items sold at ballpark concessions in America and other countries?

4. Conversation Strategies/Role Play

> When we want to introduce a suggestion or a new topic of conversation, we can use: *I'll tell you what.* ex. *I'll tell you what, if you go up and get 25 hot dogs, I, I won't fine you the 25.*

Try It

A: *announce a problem* _____.
   ex. *I'll tell you what, it is hard for me to fall asleep.*
B: *introduces a suggestion* _____.
   ex. *I'll tell you what, if you stop watching TV an hour before bedtime, it might help.*
A: *Thank you, I'll try that.*
B. *You're welcome. No problem.*

Insider Advice:
How to not get yourself in kangaroo court, newfound food

PROFILE

Name: Keiichi Yabu

Position: Right-handed pitcher

Playing experience: NPB, MLB, Mexico League. Yabu-san's career spanned 16 seasons in Japan, Mexico, and the U.S. He has had some fun times. Then again, he's a funny guy. So, no wonder!

Current job: broadcaster, YouTuber, pitching consultant

FUN FACTS

Biggest out: Struck out Derek Jeter on a 3-2 fastball.

Favorite part of playing in MLB: Hearing the American National Anthem before games. "I can sing it."

Favorite food while outside Japan: Yabu-san discovered and fell in love with burritos while playing in the U.S. and Mexico. His favorite is the egg burrito. He likes to call them "Yabu-rrito".

How to avoid kangaroo court: "I was in kangaroo court. I shaved my hair and left it in the drain. My teammates said, 'Did you do this?' I said, 'Guilty' and had to pay $45US. Don't do that."

How to learn Baseball English: Speak with your teammates. "They taught me a lot."

You can see more of Yabu-san on his YouTube channel: shorturl.at/gANR2

Discussion Questions

1. What's your favorite part of baseball?
2. Can you recommend any food that originally comes from outside of your country?
3. What question would you ask Yabu-san if you had a chance to meet him?

5. Reading Spotlight
Conor Brooks: *Keyholing*

A. Key Vocabulary Review
Here are some terms related to the reading below.
Match the terms (1-5) with the definitions (a-e).

1. ____ batting practice
2. ____ accurate
3. ____ keyhole
4. ____ advance scout
5. ____ crow hop

a. free from mistakes or errors
b. checking other teams before playing them
c. a short jump with both feet together
d. the opening in a lock into which a key is placed
e. before the game starts when a team works on its swings and hitting techniques

B. Photo Warm-Up
1. Describe what the man is doing in this photo.
2. What is the man standing behind? Why is he standing behind that?

C. Use the words from A (1-5) to complete the passage below.
Make sure to use the proper form of each word.

D. Read
Optional: Try reading aloud with a partner. Take turns reading after a sentence or two.

Former Pro Pitcher Transitions to Batting Practice (BP) Coach
An interview with Conor Brooks, current New York Mets Scout and former BP pitcher for the Texas Rangers

How did you get the job of BP pitcher?
I was contacted by the front office from the Texas Rangers asking about potential interest in a current job opening. They had received my resume from another team, who I had interviewed with and been passed over for an internship they had for 1. _____. The Rangers were looking for someone who could throw batting practice, help with advance scouting, travel with the ML team and set up the video system on the road. I had to fly to Arizona and throw batting practice to Andruw Jones and interview with the assistant GM immediately, after which he commented that, as I gave up a lot of hits in my pro career, I would be ideal for this job!

Do you have a special menu of pitches for each batter?
Not by design. Each hitter would want you to throw right down the middle every time, unless they asked for something specific. Usually that would be the bottom of the zone or the outer corner. Sometimes hitters would get upset if you didn't put it where they wanted, and they wouldn't swing unless you did. The term they called this was getting "keyholed," or "they were keyholing you." Basically, the hitter wants you to throw it to a spot as small as a 2. _____.

About how many pitches did you throw each BP?
I never thought of it in terms of total pitches. I often threw early 3. _____ before the stadium opened each team has designated times they can be on the field for "early work." I would typically throw for around 45 minutes to a group of 4-6 hitters. You probably go through 100 or so pitches in that amount of time. Sometimes I would throw a round of BP before the game—usually to the last group. That would last another 15 minutes, probably 40 pitches.

What surprised you most about the job?
Even though I was just finished with playing professionally, this wasn't a job I had much experience with and was starting from scratch in a way. I was surprised by how quickly I was forced to adjust. The team had already started Spring Training when I was hired, so I had to learn everything on the fly while also getting my arm and mind in shape for dealing with the pressure of trying to be perfect for 45 minutes a day.

Did you communicate with non-native English speaker (NNES) players in English during BP?
If so, what did you mostly talk about?
Yes, I would communicate with Spanish players in English and Spanish. We would talk about where they would want the ball thrown or how hard. "Abajo - down," "Afuera - outside," "Duro - hard" were common terms we would use, in both languages. BP was often a time native English speakers would get to learn some Spanish Baseball vernacular, and translations would often create bonding experiences with teammates.

How important is it for NNES players to learn Baseball English?
Extremely important. It's not only a tool to help NNES players do their job to the best of their ability, but it's also a way to break down social barriers for a player learning the culture in a new country. Aside from the benefits in player development from learning Baseball English, it will affect a player's confidence on a daily basis, which plays a massive part in a player's consistency and ability to play at the highest levels.

What advice do you have for someone who wants to throw BP?
Practice. I was always 4. _____ throwing things because I grew up throwing a ball against a chimney in my backyard for hours a day. Throwing a baseball to a target from 45 feet away is a good place to start. You still need to be able to block out distraction and stress, but the first requirement is to be very accurate.

Do you have a memorable story?
Throwing to Vladimir Guerrero was one of the more memorable experiences of my BP throwing career. On the last pitch of his round, he would take a 5. _____ towards the mound, shortening the distance between him and me. I was already ducking before I would release the ball because when he would make contact it would be a missile back at me!

Thanks again. One follow-up question. You said, "Vlad would take a crow hop with the bat in hand." Did he do it as a joke? He seems like a playful guy who had fun out there.
Sort of joking. He laughed as the pitcher would duck but it was more to work on being late, I think. He did it every day [as] his last swing of the day for BP.

Anything else?
It really helps to be left-handed!

D. Are the Sentences True (T) or False (F)? If False (F), Correct the Sentence.

True or False

1. Conor Brooks played for the Texas Rangers.
2. Hitters do not mind what part of the plate BP pitchers throw to them.
3. According to Conor, learning Baseball English may not help NNES players in many ways.
4. Making accurate pitches is an important part of a BP pitcher's job.
5. Conor used both Spanish and English when communicating with hitters during BP.
6. Vladimir Guerrero would take a crow hop step toward the mound when practicing a throwing technique.

Conor Brooks throws BP at Fenway Park

E. Talk TIME

1. How does this phrase apply to Conor Brooks: When one door closes, another opens?
2. Opinion: What are two interesting things you learned from this interview?
3. What are some languages that are important to learn for baseball? Rank them from 1-3 and explain.
4. For BP pitchers, why do you think it is important to be left-handed?

UNIT 3

Pitching: A Large Percent Of The Game

Topics: Pitching vocabulary, Grips, Off-speed challenge, Controversial remarks

1. Batter Up! Vocabulary

A. Guess the Meaning of Each Photo

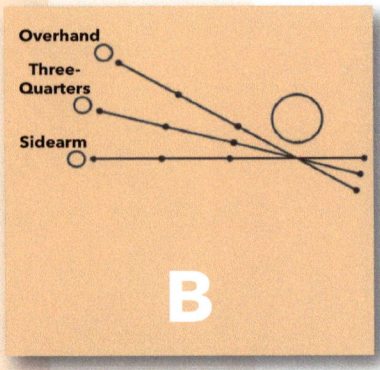
B

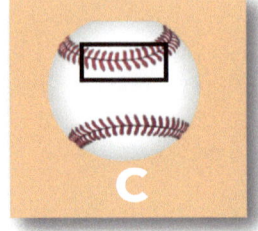
C

D

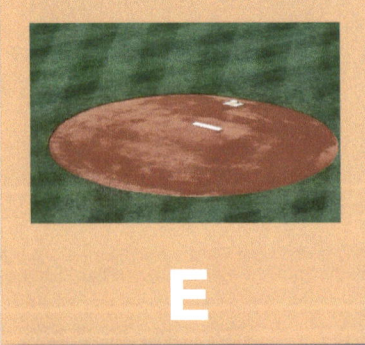
E

F

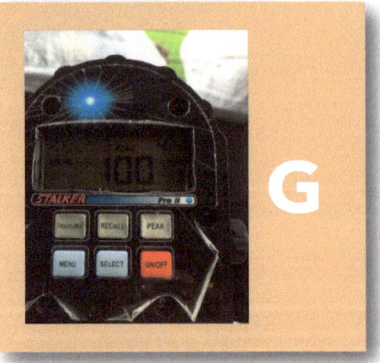
G

H

I

J

K

L

M

B. Talkin' Photos
Discuss the photos Try speaking in complete sentences

C. Match Each Photo With a Vocabulary Term
- bullpen
- mound
- pickoff
- rubber
- curve/curveball
- seam(s)
- long toss
- velocity/velo
- strike
- strikeout
- arm slot/arm angle
- release point
- strike zone/zone

D. Match Each Arm Slot/Angle Photo With a Vocabulary Term.

1. ____ sidearm
2. ____ three-quarter (3/4)
3. ____ overhand/overhead

E. Match Each Pitching Grip Photo With a Vocabulary Term.

a   b   c   d   e

1. Fastballs
Match each grip photo with a vocabulary term.
1. ____ forkball
2. ____ four-seam/seamer fastball
3. ____ two-seam/seamer fastball
4. ____ cutter/cut/cut fastball
5. ____ split/splitter/split finger fastball

Off-Speed Challenge! **Breaking Balls, Changeups, and Junk**

2. Breaking Balls
Match each grip photo with a vocabulary term.

1. ____ curve/curveball
2. ____ slider
3. ____ slurve

G. Match Each Grip Photo With a Vocabulary Term.

> **3. Changeups and Junk**
> *Match each grip photo with a vocabulary term.*
>
> 1. ____ knuckleball
> 2. ____ knuckle curve
> 3. ____ changeup/change
> 4. ____ circle change/changeup
>
> a   b   c   d
>
>

2. Vocabulary Exercises

A. Collocation Match-Up:
Match the two parts of these phrases.

1. ____ move   a. arm
2. ____ stretch   b. pitch
3. ____ pitcher   c. the
4. ____ side   d. inside
5. ____ count   e. right-handed

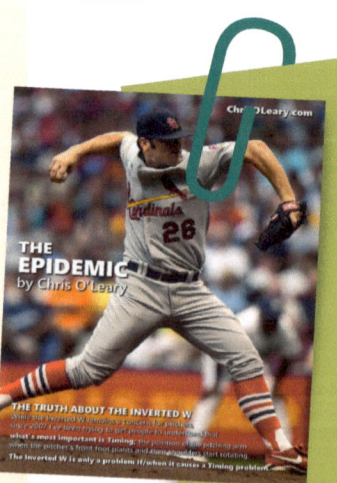

Insider Advice: The Inverted W

Recently, the Inverted W **arm action**, has created discussion of whether it causes shoulder and/or elbow injuries to **pitchers**. For extensive reading about this, you can check out these studies on the Internet by: ChrisOLeary.com, TopVelocity.net, and Driveline.com.

Also, some research shows a relationship between injuries and the use of certain **arm slots** or **arm angles** such as sidearm. Learning about this may help prevent injuries.

1. Which professional pitchers have you watched use the **Inverted W**?
2. Have they suffered extensive shoulder or elbow injuries?

B. Cluster Challenge:
Complete the collocations using these words:
velocity/count/release/first/spin/strikeout/ball/move/effective/slot/pickoff

1. A situation in which you use the inside _____ is going to be runners on first and second or bases loaded, two outs, full count.
2. Now, for you guys who are a little bit higher on your arm _____ , I definitely recommend a hard curve or a sharp slider that has more downward break than side-to-side.
3. The best pickoff move to first base is going to be the _____ move.
4. A slider is a very _____ pitch for deceiving the batter.
5. A pitching _____ killer is pulling the glove down.
6. We want to keep that pitch _____ down—we have a lot of games to go.
7. Typically, it's going to be a _____ pitch because it looks like a fastball, and then, in the last five feet or so, it breaks off the table to make it a slider.
8. You'll see a lot of the high-velocity pitchers, when they get to this point, they'll actually straighten that front leg out as they're coming to their _____ point.
9. If you have it too loose, you'll tend to leave the _____ up in the zone and we all know, as pitchers, those balls usually don't come back.
10. Let's talk about _____ moves to third base for right-handed pitchers. What we got, obviously, just like the other ones, just like first base and second base, we've got our step off. Okay, once we step off, we do not have to throw; we can do whatever we want.
11. I just think he is going to swing at the _____ pitch…alright, come on, good body language.

C. Skill Practice:
Complete each sentence said by managers or coaches, using the given vocabulary terms below.

1. So, if you want to get a little more break, throw that knuckle on there and it'll get a different _____ but you should still have the same feel.
   a. spin b. ball c. strike
2. Player A: How'd you pitch?
   Player B: It was good, 1, 2, 3, _____ on the last guy, 95 on the black. Works, I guess.
   a. high b. strikeout c. ball
3. Would you throw a _____ seven days a week, or even six days a week? No chance!
   a. strike b. curve c. bullpen
4. Yeah, nice _____ . Speak up, ump!
   a. wild b. first c. pitch

5. Scientifically, we know that _____ toss and weighted ball programs put as much or more stress on the arm as pitching off the mound.
   a. long b. soft c. underhand

6. Some people theorize that you shouldn't throw a _____ ball until you can shave to take the stress off of the elbow.
   a. foul b. Wiffle c. breaking

7. So, we want to create some _____ and timing, we take that drop step, we stay on the ball of the foot and then we go ahead and reach out with our stride foot to our landing.
   a. rhythm b. victories c. off-speed

8. You work off of location and also off of breaking _____ and off-speed _____ fastballs as well, but location is very important.
   a. stuff b. hits c. types

9. No matter where you throw, like how you throw—sidearm, anything—you want everything to look like your fastball. Every single arm _____ , every single pitch needs to look like your fastball.
   a. injury b. side c. action

10. The thing is, high school players often play many positions, so they have to find a comfortable arm _____ that they can use regardless of the position that they play on defense.
    a. speed b. slot c. bar

3. Insider Baseball Talk

Mound Talk. Listen as pitching coach Buddy York makes a mound visit to speak with pitcher Dumas Garcia.

A. Photo Warm-Up
1. Describe the photo.
2. How do you think the pitcher feels? Why?

B. Watch and Listen-In
(Video 5)

Please go to www.sportsEnglish.org/media

Optional: Focus on watching the video at least one time before completing the gap-filling exercise on the next page.

pitcher

C. Gap-Filling: Watch the Video and Fill in the Blanks With the Vocabulary You Hear.

> **Coach Buddy York:**
> Hey, here we go. Just _____ down a little bit.
> Let's get after him. _____ ball, we're back in business.
> Flyball, we're back in _____ . Anything you got right here—
> strikeout. _____ we gotta do. Alright?

D. Key Vocabulary

Match the words that have similar meanings.
Use the dialogue (C) to help with context clues.

1. calm down   2. ground   3. gotta   4. hey   5. whatever
a. must   b. everything   c. relax   d. dirt   e. hello

E. Discussion Questions
1. Why do you think Buddy came to the mound?
2. Do you think Buddy gave the pitcher good advice? Why or why not?

Idiom Focus
Back in Business

Notice in video 5 how Coach Buddy explains to the pitcher, Dumas Garcia, that a fly ball or ground ball will get the team *"back in business"*. This means that the team will be okay after the pitcher got in a bad situation. In this case, the pitcher allowed runners to get on base, which is not good. You can use *back in business* in baseball or general English.

Example: After feeling sick for the last week, I am *back in business*.

F. Conversation Strategy/Coaching Role Play: *Back in business*
Try It:
Pretend you are a baseball coach. Use *back in business* when speaking with a player. Write your answers below.

Example: *Hey, you went 3 for 4 with a home run last night. You're back in business!*

1. _____
   _____

2. _____
   _____

4. Everyday English: "Hang in there."

Listen to the manager make a pitching change.

A. Photo Warm-Up
1. Discuss the photo. Try to speak in complete sentences.
   ex. *It looks like they…*
2. What do you think Wally is doing?
3. Why do you think Wally has his hand on the player's (#31) back?

B. Watch and Listen-In (Video 6)
Please go to www.sportsEnglish.org/media

Optional: Focus on watching the video at least one time before completing the gap-filling exercise below.

C. Gap-Filling:
Watch the video and fill in the blanks with the vocabulary you hear.

Wally: Hang in there, _____ _____ .
Wally: Hang in there, _____ .

D. Practice
Read aloud what Wally said to the player.

E. General English Vocabulary
Match each term with its meaning.

1. ___ big guy   a. friend
2. ___ buddy   b. term of endearment toward an overall good male

F. Discussion Questions
1. What does *hang in there* mean?
2. Why did Wally say *hang in there* to the player?
3. What else could Wally have said to this player?
4. How do you think the player, #31, felt?

Hang in there is commonly heard in Baseball and Sports English, but also in everyday English. It is used as:

an expression of encouragement to persist or stay calm in a challenging situation. The player in the video, #31, had just pitched poorly and Wally, his manager, used *hang in there* in a positive, uplifting way.

By saying *buddy* or *big guy* to *hang in there,* Wally tried to encourage the player after a difficult performance. You could also use *friend*, *man*, *girl*, *dude*– all terms of endearment. You may also use their name. Ex. Hang in there, Jeff.

G. Conversation Strategies
Try It:
With a partner, try using hang in there, and add a term of endearment, ex. buddy or the person's name, to the end of a sentence.
Ex. *A: I walked 10 (batters) yesterday.*
   B: Hang in there, _____ .

   A: My girlfriend broke up with me.
   B. Hang in there, _____ .

Did You Know?
Unique Story About a Special Player

Hideo Nomo, nicknamed "The Tornado" for his unique windup and delivery, retired from Japan's NPB at age 25 to sign a minor league deal with the Los Angeles Dodgers. Nomo pitched the first month of the 1995 season in the minor leagues before getting called up. Fred Claire, the general manager who signed him recalls a unique story about Nomo:

"When the 1995 season began, Hideo was not on the active roster but it was very clear that he wanted to be in uniform and part of the Opening Day introductions. It showed me that he had a sense of how his journey in the Major Leagues was going to be examined in every way and in every detail. Hideo from the beginning understood his place in baseball [and] Japan's baseball history."
-Fred Claire, Los Angeles Dodgers GM (1987-1998)

1. What does this story tell you about Hideo Nomo as a professional baseball player?
2. Do you agree with Nomo's request to be in uniform and part of Opening Day ceremonies when he was not on the active roster? Why or why not?

5. Reading Spotlight

Shane Youman Interview: An incident to learn from
"No matter your ethnic background, you will either feel hurt, anger, or both when it comes to racism towards you."

A. Warm-Up
1. What is racism?
2. Do you think racism exists in sports? If yes, provide an example.
3. Have you said something that hurt another person's feelings and then realized that you made a mistake? Explain.

A. Key Vocabulary
Here are some terms related to the reading below. Match the terms (1-6) with the definitions (a-f).

1. ___ nationality
2. ___ racist
3. ___ remarks
4. ___ slugger
5. ___ netizens
6. ___ controversy

a. something that someone says to express an opinion or idea
b. a player who hits the baseball very hard
c. people who actively use the Internet
d. an argument that involves many people who strongly disagree about something
e. a group of people who share the same history, traditions, and language, and who usually live together in a particular country
f. poor treatment of, or violence against, people because of their race

B. Use the Terms From A (1-6) to Complete the Passage Below

C. Read
This news article is courtesy of Jeff Liebsch, Haps Magazine.

Optional: Try reading aloud with a partner. Take turns reading after a sentence or two.

Shane Youman

Exclusive Interview: American Pitcher Shane Youman Reacts to Controversial Remarks

By Jeff Liebsch, Haps Magazine – www.hapskorea.com – June 12, 2013

BUSAN, South Korea – It's been an interesting 24 hours for Lotte Giants pitcher Shane Youman. The 33-year-old starting pitcher from New Iberia, Louisiana unsuspectedly was at the center of controversy yesterday, when Hanwha Eagles' 1 _____ Kim Tae-kyun was asked during an appearance on an Internet baseball radio broadcast about difficulties batting with the Giants' ace on the mound.

The star Korean slugger replied:
"The Lotte Giants' Youman is the most difficult player to play against. His face is too black, so it is hard to bat because his white teeth and the ball confuses me when he smiles on the mound. So, I suffered a lot."

He then went on to add, "There's no particularly difficult pitcher, but when I play against Youman, I screw up because of his white teeth."

An eruption of negative comments ensued on Korean baseball forums as Korean 2 _____ charged Kim with making 3 _____ statements. The outpouring from fans caused both Kim and the Eagles to immediately issue personal apologies to Youman.

In an exclusive e-mail interview with Haps, Youman gives his take on the comments, the 4 _____ and to baseball life for an African-American journeyman in Korea.

What was your reaction when you first heard Kim's comments about you? Has there been any time when you felt your race or nationality played a role in how you were treated during your time playing here?
After hearing about Kim Tae-kyun from my translator initially I laughed, and said it was OK, not a problem, people make mistakes. After I thought about it for a bit, I became a little upset, which is the initial reaction from someone who hears about something that's potentially racist towards them. No matter your ethnic background, you will either feel hurt, anger, or both when it comes to racism towards you.

As far as being here in Korea, I've never felt that my race or 5 _____ has played a role in how I've been treated. Then again, I'd never know, because I don't speak Korean (lol).

Korean netizens were very vocal in your defense, calling Kim's comments racist. What is your feeling on their response to Kim's 6 _____ about facing you from the batter's box?
Knowing that fans and friends here have been very vocal in defending me is very appreciated. However, after more pondering, I really feel that he made a big mistake, perhaps trying to be funny not thinking about the consequences of his words. Only Kim Tae-kyun knows.

I feel that the majority of the folks here in Korea may not fully understand what racism is, or what can come off as being racist, because most people here haven't fully experienced it, or probably don't know anyone that has. Kim Tae-kyun I feel is part of that majority. I will again say that, I really do appreciate the natives of Korea, and others who are in support of me in this situation.

What kind of reaction do you think would have happened had this occurred to a minority player in the US?
I'm sure in the US it would be much of the same type of reaction, but perhaps a little more, because people in the states are more aware of what racism, or being racist really is.

How did the team handle the situation, and how do you think the media handled it?
As far as the team goes, no one has really said anything to me about this issue. That was really surprising to me, being that I'm part of the Lotte brand. Who knows as to why they haven't spoken to me, yet.

The Giants will host the Eagles here in Busan this weekend. Any idea on how your meeting with Kim will go?
How ironic is it that we will host Hanwha this weekend? I'm sure things will heat up a bit with the Lotte fans (gotta love 'em). I will remain focused on my job, but we both know this incident will be something in the back of my mind. I'm just going to be interested to hear the reception Kim Tae-kyun gets not only in his first at-bat, but throughout the entire series.

The front of the shirt says "Be careful what you say," which accompanies the message on the back, which reads "Someone is listening."

UPDATE

A year after the Kim incident and other occurrences of controversial remarks made inside Korean baseball toward others, Youman created a custom-made t-shirt to raise awareness about racism in the sport. Shane hosts the League Talk Podcast and helps young athletes at his academy, TruYou Athletics in Fort Worth, Texas, USA.

D. Read and Answer the Following Quiz Questions
1. Who pitched for the Lotte Giants?
2. What caused the controversy described above?
3. Who made comments that upset Shane Youman and people from Busan?
4. What does netizens mean? Are you a netizen?
5. What did Shane Youman do to raise awareness about racism in Korean baseball?
6. How can racism be avoided?

UNIT 4 — Out In The Field

Topics: Infield, Outfield, "I got it!", Meet-and-greet, A woman saving victims: Coaching in Cambodia

1. Batter Up! Vocabulary

A. Guess the Meaning of Each Photo Below

A

B

C

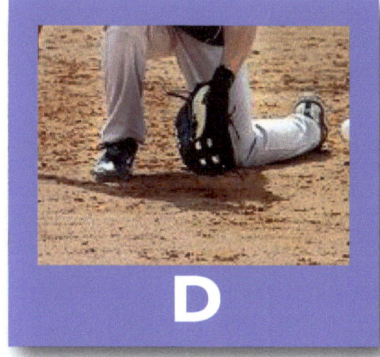

D

E

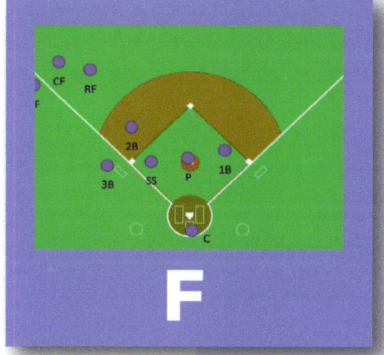

F

G

H

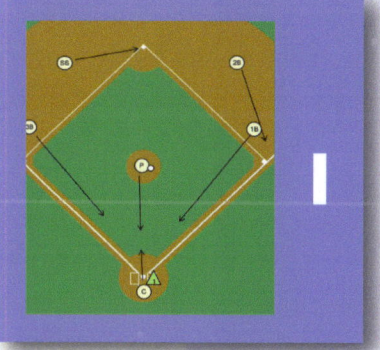

I

J

K

L

B. Talkin' Photos on page 37
Discuss the photos Try speaking in complete sentences

C. Match Each Photo With a Vocabulary Term (A. page 37)

- baseball field/field
- bunt defense
- fly ball
- flat glove
- crow hop
- tag
- infield drill
- (the) shift
- ground ball
- catcher
- snow cone (catch)
- backhand

2. Field Work

A. Write the term next to the position or part of the field.

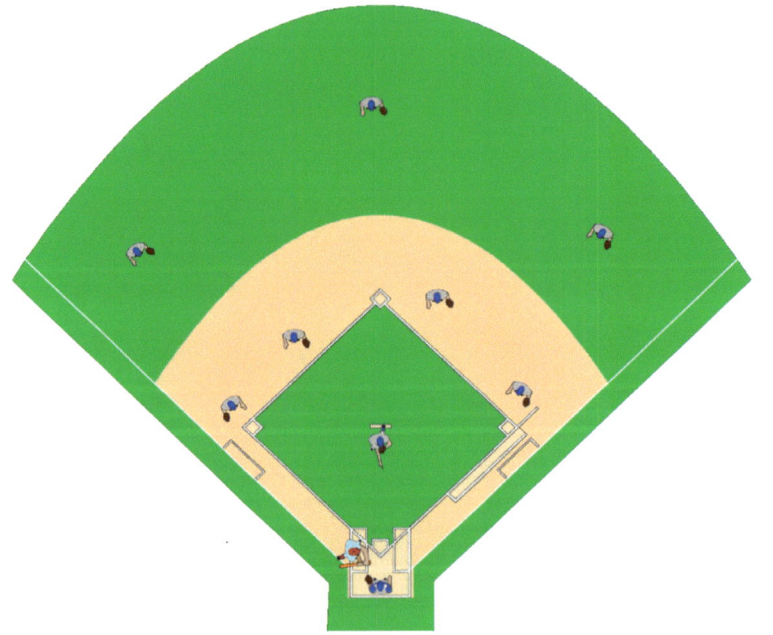

1. catcher
2. first baseman/woman
3. hitter
4. plate
5. infield
6. outfield
7. second baseman/woman
8. right field
9. short/shortstop
10. third baseman/woman
11. center field
12. middle infielders
13. right field line
14. left field
15. right center

BONUS: Circle the power positions.

B. Choose a famous player for each position and discuss with a partner.
Ex. *Yu Darvish is a pitcher.*

3. Vocabulary

A. Collocation Match-Up: Match the two parts of these phrases.

1. ___ position   a. weak
2. ___ mitt   b. first
3. ___ ball   c. center
4. ___ base   d. power
5. ___ protector   e. infield
6. ___ infielder   f. double
7. ___ field   g. chest
8. ___ hands   h. fly
9. ___ ground ball   i. middle
10. ___ play   j. quick

B. Cluster Challenge:
Complete the collocations using these words:
glove/infield/out/tag/backhand/footwork/shift/outfield/catcher/field

1. I sometimes can't see the _____ 's fingers because of where the sun is or if they have their legs closed to keep the batter and base runner from seeing the sign.

2. He put down the _____ . He's out!

3. _____ it with one hand; get this shoulder to first base.

4. One thing I notice when I watch you play is the size of your _____ ; you use a big one for a third baseman.

5. Usually they try to put the _____ on the infield.

6. If I am an outfielder, my _____ is more exaggerated or longer; I can go ahead and get a little bit more arm arc and get it a little bit higher so I can work down on top of the baseball to make my long throws.

7. Going to the _____ , forehand, regular ground ball, it doesn't matter, I want to catch the ball out in front here.

8. We will take _____ at 5:50 PM.

9. Throwing _____ a baserunner isn't done with the strength of our arms but the quickness of our feet.

10. When you are in the _____ shagging, you don't have to be gung-ho about it, but be professional about it and get the job done.

C. Skill Practice:

Complete each naturally spoken sentence using the given vocabulary terms below.

1. When we get to a point where we are throwing long, at that point, this step-through is going to become the first part of my _____ . We always want to create a little bit of energy and momentum toward our target to help us get our body turned correctly.
   a. jab step b. short hop c. crow hop

2. The most important thing on a _____ ball is trying to hit, you know, your _____ partner right in the chest.
   a. double play b. long hop c. glove action

3. When you are going back for a _____ , that ball tends to bounce up and down on you; you really have to work on staying on your toes, controlling your breathing, everything. That way, if the ball starts bouncing, you can make an easy catch.
   a. fly ball b. long throw c. line drive

4. For those who don't understand what the shortstop and the _____ are doing when you see them cover their mouth with the glove, they are letting each other know who is going to cover second base if there is a runner at first base stealing a base.
   a. center fielder b. first baseman/woman c. second baseman/woman

5. He had him in a _____ or pickle.
   a. bullpen b. foul territory c. rundown

6. The _____ that MLB has in effect is, in a lot of ways, intended to protect the infielders, having to stay at the base.
   a. neighborhood play b. fair ball c. jab step

Did You Know?

The *power positions* (PP) in baseball are positions in which players typically manufacture the most offensive POWER. Historically, first base has produced the most power, but recently an MLB statistic (OPS+) indicated that third base and first base are nearly equal.

1. What are some other PP?
2. What positions are usually not PP?
3. Which position do you think requires the most defensive skills? Why?

To learn more about this recent shift in PP:
https://www.espn.com/mlb/story/_/id/25459266/is-third-base-passing-first-base-baseball-power-position

4. Insider Baseball Talk: Ball hog!

Let's go to the infield and watch a fun moment as Joey Hooft calls Desi Wilson off a pop-up.

Photo Warm-Up
Describe the photo and discuss it with others.

A. Watch and Listen-In 1 (Video 7)
Please go to www.sportsEnglish.org/media
Optional: Focus on watching the video at least one time before completing the gap-filling exercise below.

B. Gap-Filling:
Watch the video and fill in the blanks with the vocabulary you hear.

Joey:	I _____ _____ , Desi!
Desi:	_____ , you got it.
Joey:	laughs
Desi:	Is it *(the microphone Joey is wearing)* on?
Joey:	Yeah, right here.
Desi:	_____ _____ !
Joey:	laughs

C. Pair Work
1. Research and discuss any unfamiliar vocabulary from the video.
2. Practice the conversation with a partner.

D. Discussion Questions
1. What is a ball hog?
2. Do you think Joey and Desi have a good relationship?
3. Why do Joey and Desi laugh?
4. Would you call your teammate a ball hog? Why
5. Is calling your teammate a funny name even if joking acceptable in your country's baseball culture?

Did You Know?

Amongst infielders and outfielders, players must yell loudly to establish who will catch a ball that is close to them! In the case with Joey, he yelled, "I got it" and his teammate's name, Desi. Some players will just say *got it* three or four times.

1. When calling for a fly ball or pop-up, which do you prefer to use or hear? Why?
   Note: To establish good communication, it's a good idea to ask your teammates to use the same term when calling for a ball.
2. Why would a player say *got it* many times when calling off another fielder?

> GOT IT: Multi-Meaning Term

E. Conversation Strategy/Role Play

Sometimes baseball terms can be used in everyday situations off the field. Notice that Joey used *got it* when calling off or telling Desi to stop going for the pop-up. We can also use *got it* to let someone know that we understand something they said or to check for understanding.

Example 1:
Coach: Let's work on a hitting drill today to build muscle memory.
Player: *Got it!*

Example 2:
Coach: If we do what we are supposed to do, it doesn't matter who we play. We'll have success. *Got it?*

Got it can also be used in place of *you're welcome* after someone thanks you for something.

Example 3: Person 1: Alright big man, thanks a lot, Jim.
Person 2: *You got it.*

1. Role play: Stand up with your partner and imagine that a pop-up or fly ball is hit your way. Call off your partner using *got it!* or *I got it!* Say it loudly and with authority. Take turns.

2. With a partner, create a short exchange similar to any of the examples from above (1-3). Practice the exchange with your partner.

5. Everyday English: Meet-and-Greet

"You throw gas?"
Part of professional baseball is fan relations. It's helpful to learn how players interact with fans. Let's listen in as South Georgia Peanuts players Chris and Mike spend time in the local community meeting a fan.

A

B

A. Photo Warm-Up
1. Describe each photo. Try to speak in complete sentences
2. In photo A, who do you think wrote on this photo?
3. In photo B, what do you think the boy and baseball players are saying?

B. Watch and Listen-In (Video 8)
Please go to www.sportsEnglish.org/media

Optional: Focus on watching the video at least one time before completing the gap-filling exercise below.

C. Gap-Filling:
Using the terms in exercise D, watch the video and fill in the blanks with the vocabulary you hear.

Chris:	So, what's your name?
Cody:	Cody.
Chris:	I'm Chris. Nice to meet you, _____ . This is Mike.
Mike:	I'm Mike. How you doing?
Cody:	Nice to meet you.
Chris:	How old are you?
Cody:	I'm eleven.
Chris:	_____ ? What position do you play?
Cody:	Um.
Chris:	Everywhere?
Cody:	Pitcher, shortstop, _____ _____ , infield.
Chris:	_____ , all over, huh?
Mike:	You throw gas?
Cody:	Huh?
Mike:	You throw hard?
Cody:	I'm only good at _____ .
Mike:	You throw sliders right now?!
Cody:	Yes.
Mike:	You're going to hurt your elbow.
Chris:	He (Cody) said it just _____ _____ .
Mike:	Oh.
Chris:	Would you like this?
Cody:	Yes, _____ . Thank you!
Chris:	You're welcome. I'm going to get you a ball when you come to the game. How's that?
Mike:	Alright, buddy.
Chris:	Thank you all for coming. One _____ fan.
Mike:	In two hours of sitting here.

D. Key Vocabulary

Match the terms and definitions with how they were used during the meet-and-greet above (C). Use the conversation to help with context clues.

1. ___ buddy
2. ___ naturally
3. ___ elbow
4. ___ sir
5. ___ cuts
6. ___ loyal

a. joint where your arm bends
b. having complete and constant support for something
c. an informal way to address a man or boy whom you do not know
d. something is expected or normal
e. to turn sharply
f. a polite way to address a man you do not know

E. Discussion Questions

1. If you have a chance, do you want to do a meet-and-greet with fans? Why or why not?
2. What's another way to say "throw gas"?
3. Why was Mike surprised that Cody throws sliders?
4. What does Chris give to Cody as a present?
5. Do you think Cody is polite? Why or why not?

F. Practice

Read aloud the conversation between Cody and the players with partners.

G. Conversation Strategies: "Nice to meet you."

> **Meet-and-Greet Tips:** making the fans feel important
> *"It's nice to be important, but it's more important to be nice."*
> *-John Templeton*

- "So, what's your name?" When introducing yourself to someone for the first time in a meet-and-greet, it's okay to ask a fan their name. This may make them feel important because a baseball player (maybe someone they highly respect and even idolize) wants to know their name.

- "I'm Chris. Nice to meet you, buddy." Notice how Chris also calls Cody "buddy," perhaps because he is younger. Also, Chris can sense that Cody looks up to him. Because Chris calls Cody buddy, a term used for friends, Cody will likely feel relaxed and perhaps even more important.

- Note: It's okay to use buddy for boys and girls. For girls, you might want to try *gal pal*. However, some people may not like names such as *buddy* or even *dude* (for boys), and *gal pal*, or *dudette* (for girls), so you could just say their name. You can also ask the person what their name is.

Try It Try using: *"So, what's your name"?* and
"Nice to meet you, buddy or gal-pal" with a partner.
A: So, what's your name?
B. I'm _____ .
A: I'm _____ .
A: Nice to meet you buddy/gal-pal.

6. Reading Spotlight

Women in Baseball: Cambodian National Team coach helps human trafficking victims
"I'm American and so I don't fall into the Cambodian woman role, but I'm also fighting for the women."

A. Warm-Up
1. What do you know about human trafficking?
2. Describe a good coach.
3. Does it matter if your coach is a man or a woman? Explain your answer.

B. Key Vocabulary
Here are some terms related to the reading below. Match the terms (1-6) with the definitions (a-f).

1. ___ psychiatric
2. ___ monk
3. ___ honor
4. ___ federation
5. ___ intense
6. ___ fastpitch

a. member of a religious community of men who usually promise to remain poor, unmarried, and separated from the rest of society
b. a type of softball, featuring higher speed and underhand pitching
c. respect that is given to someone who is admired
d. a branch of medicine dealing with mental or emotional disorders
e. an organization formed by joining several groups or parties
f. done with or showing great energy, enthusiasm, or effort

C. Use the Terms From A (1-6) to Complete the Passage

D. Read
Read excerpts from an interview on the Coming to America Baseball Podcast hosted by Philip Riccobono, with guest Jessica Neitz, a member of the Cambodia Baseball 1._____ who operates a rescue mission, coaches for the men's national team, and is manager of the women's national team.

45

continued from page 45

So, I want to start off by saying baseball is definitely important in our lives, but I think you and your family are doing something that's extraordinary. Can you tell us about your life in Cambodia?

Jessica: Yeah. We've been here eight years…we have our home, Esther's House. It has about 24 girls now. All have been brought in from some pretty horrible situations. When they come to us, obviously, they're given immediate medical attention and then 2._____ attention as well. We kind of bring them through the physical and mental healing.

Interviewer: How did you and your husband [start Esther's House]? I mean, was this a calling? This is amazing.

Jessica: A lady we met in Africa said, "You'll know where you're supposed to be because when you see the children's faces, you won't be able to forget them." We got off the plane [in Cambodia] and immediately just fell in love with the country and the kids.

I had met you last year [2019] in the Philippines at the Southeast Games (SEA). I was surprised to see a female coach for a men's national baseball team. I've never seen it before in my life, but I've seen Justine Siegal with the Oakland A's as a special assignment coach, and now Alyssa Nakken, the first full-time female coach in MLB with the San Francisco Giants. And then there's Jessica Neitz. How did this all happen?

Jessica: So, I told you, we work with little kids and something outside of just this, you'll go crazy and it'll tear you apart. So, we did something as a family just to kind of take our mind off of it, give us an out. And my son, an avid baseball player, loves the sport, loves playing. I grew up playing. My husband grew up playing. I played baseball up until, I think, sixth Grade. The coach there was like, "You've made the team, but the girls your age are really starting to get into 3._____ softball." I begged him. I said, "No, no, no." My experience at that point wasn't a very high experience of the game, and I really loved baseball. But I took a suggestion and went and tried out for a team and just absolutely loved it, fell in love with the sport. There are more opportunities for females with fastpitch softball. So, our family just kind of grew up with the sport. I got on Facebook and just kind of said, "If baseball wasn't here in Cambodia," then we were like, "let's start baseball here in Cambodia." But we saw a Facebook group and I'm like, "Well, let's not recreate, let's just reach out and see how we can help." And that's when we met the president of the organization. He put us as the coaches of a local high school club. So, we started there and just worked with these young men. We have, I think, about 600 players now, which is a low number but it's growing.

How do you and Takashi-san [Cambodia National Men's team manager] communicate, because you have three languages going on there—English, Japanese, and Khmer?

Jessica: Takashi could speak bits and phrases of English, but we use Google Translate.

I'll never forget this. Your guys were in the field and your pitcher was, like, maybe 120 pounds soaking wet, throwing a 55, 60 mile per hour fastball. But [at the beginning of the game] every time they made an out, they took their hats off and waved them like they had won the World Series. It was great. It was so nice to see that enthusiasm. That was awesome!

Jessica: To be a part of that, I mean, it was such an 4._____ to be asked to—when I was asked to help out with the national team, never did I think that I would be asked to go to the SEA Games. Maybe two or three players, none of them ever left Cambodia before. And so—a plane, going into another country, playing baseball in another country, that was all new to them. So, it was exciting. Yeah, the energy they brought to that first game was pretty 5._____ … I wish we had won a game.

Do your players follow MLB? Do they have heroes? Do they know Mike Trout? Do they follow Japanese baseball?

Jessica: They follow both [MLB and Japanese baseball]. The ones that are invested in the sport and really trying to get better, they're streaming YouTube all the time.

English is important in baseball. Do they have to know that?

Jessica: We encourage that at our umpire training. I hate to say this, but if anybody wants a future in baseball, you have to speak the [English] language. Some of the players knew English. I mean, we had told the Cambodia Baseball Federation that, but there is a lack of education in Cambodia. In fact, one of our best players, he played second base and a little bit of outfield. And then during COVID, his parents basically told him, "If you don't go to school, then you need to go be a 6._____." And he quit and now he's a monk. He was 16 years old, probably one of the better players in Cambodia. And just because he didn't want to go to school, he became a monk. And so now we're trying to find him and get him out of that.

continued from page 47

Well, that's interesting. That's a good story. This gives a good perspective of what it's like to coach in Cambodia.

Jessica: [Also], females are not looked here as highly—in America, there are a lot more opportunities. In a country where men are taught that females have a certain role, when they come in and obviously, I'm white and I'm American and so I don't fall into the Cambodian woman role, but I'm also fighting for the women. I've been named the national head coach for the women's team.

Oh, cool. I didn't even know they had a team.
Jessica: Yeah, well, we did until COVID hit.

Can you tell me about the women's national team? So, you've been named manager of the women's national team. When did this happen and what's going on?
Jessica: Basically, they [the Cambodia Baseball Federation] called me. When I was in the Philippines, because we didn't have a team at that point that could compete, I did do a little bit of scouting to see where the [Cambodian] women are compared to other countries.

To contact Jessica or donate to Esther's House, go to www.esthershouserescue.org. The full interview is available at www.ComingToAmericaBaseball.com or www.YouTube.com/ComingToAmericaBB.

E. Are the Sentences True (T) or False (F)?
If False, Correct the Sentence.

True or False

1. Jessica Neitz has lived in Cambodia her whole life.
2. Jessica and her family chose to live in Cambodia.
3. Jessica started baseball in Cambodia.
4. Cambodian baseball won the 2019 SEA Games
5. Cambodia's baseball players now follow MLB.
6. English is not really necessary to work in baseball.

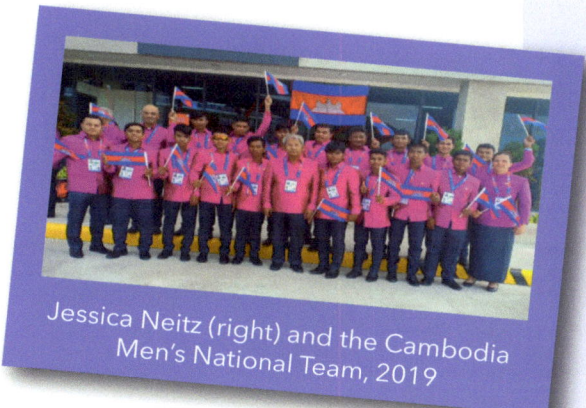

Jessica Neitz (right) and the Cambodia Men's National Team, 2019

Talk TIME

F. Read and Answer the Following Questions.
Then Discuss Your Answers in a Group.

1. How does Jessica help people in Cambodia?
2. Does Jessica inspire you? Why or why not?
3. Do you agree that "if anybody wants a future in baseball, you have to speak the [English] language"? Why or why not?
4. Why do you feel the Cambodia Baseball Federation chose Jessica to serve as a coach on the men's national team and name her as manager of the women's national team?
5. What challenges does Jessica face as a baseball coach in Cambodia? Explain.
6. Would you consider coaching or working in another country where baseball is not so popular and is growing? Where? Why?

Hitter-Runner: Batter Up!

Topics: Hitting, Running, Too much spin, The sweet spot, Slump, Bunt, Tag up, A lost art

1. Batter Up! Vocabulary

A. Name as many items as you can in each photo, *ex. There's a bat.*

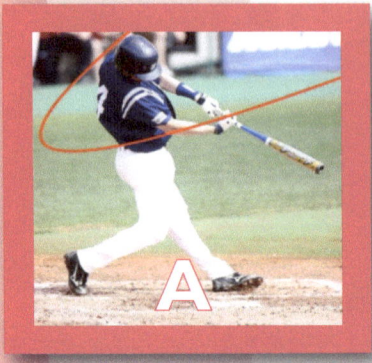
A

B

C

D

E

F

G

H

I

J

K

L

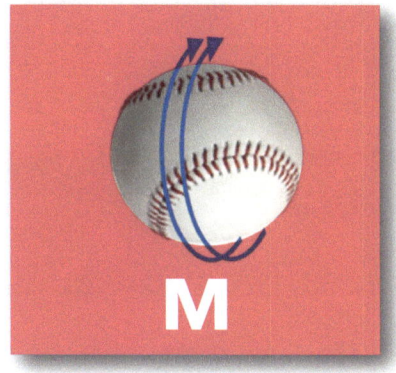
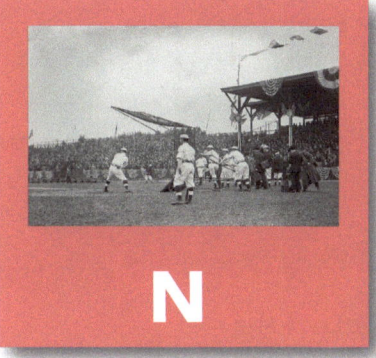

M   N   O

B. Talkin' Photos
Discuss the photos Try speaking in complete sentences

C. Work Alone or With a partner to Label Each Photo
1. tee
2. stride foot
3. cages/batting cages
4. slide
5. BP/batting practice
6. topspin
7. extension
8. bat/swing path
9. lead
10. backspin
11. tag, tag, tag!
12. front toss drill
13. contact point
14. base stealer
15. soft toss drill

D. Put the Above Terms in the Correct Column

Hitting   Running

Did You Know?
Less Spin = More Home Runs

Spin rate matters for both pitching and hitting. According to FiveThirtyEight.com, "when too much spin is added at certain launch angles, there is a 'ballooning' effect. For baseball hitters, that means that too much spin might lead to batted balls traveling higher, but not farther." However, in a 2019 study, FiveThirtyEight.com found that "*exit velocity* off the bat was at a record level since Statcast began ball-tracking in 2015, but that year spin rate has actually *declined*, according to Statcast data analyzed by FiveThirtyEight." This study suggests less backspin from pitching resulted in a record 6776 home runs for the 2019 MLB season.

Does more backspin (on the baseball) favor the hitter or pitcher? Why?

E. Know Your Bat!
1. Write each term below on the area of the bat to which it belongs.
barrel/knob/bat head/handle

Discussion Questions
1. What is the sweet spot of a baseball or softball bat?
2. Where is the sweet spot on a bat?

Did You Know? (Where the Sweet Spot Is)?

"There is no single definition of the sweet spot for a baseball or softball bat. There are locations on the barrel which result in maximum performance and there are locations which result in minimal discomfort in the hands. **These locations are not the same for a given bat, and there is considerable variation in locations between bats.**"

Source: *Physics and Acoustics of Baseball & Softball Bats,* by Daniel A. Russell, Ph.D. (2003)

Take a Closer Look
Which former MLB slugger used this bat? Why is this bat so special?

Mark McGwire used this bat during the 1998 season when he broke Roger Maris' HR record (62 in a season). McGwire hit 70 in '98. A few years later (2001), Barry Bonds passed the mark with 73.

F. Stances
Match each batting stance type with the photo.

a   b   c

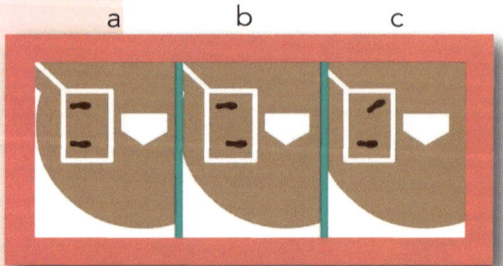

1. open stance   ____
2. closed stance   ____
3. normal/square stance ____

Insider Advice
Choose your stance. Pick between the neutral, open, and closed stances. Base your decision partly on whichever one makes it easier to keep your dominant eye on the ball. Also consider how the placement of your feet in each position affects your swing. In addition, you may need to adjust your stance based on whether the pitcher is throwing fast or slow. Regardless of which one you choose, bend your knees a little. Point your toes toward the plate with your feet spread shoulder-width or a few inches wider.
Normal/neutral stance (also called "even stance"): *Both feet are placed an equal distance from home plate. This is the most popular stance because*

it allows you to turn your head over your shoulder without any strain so that you can face the pitcher and keep both eyes on the ball.
Open stance: *The foot closest to the pitcher is moved slightly back so that the front of your body is a little more "open" to the pitcher. This is the least popular stance because it takes you out of hitting position, thus creating extra steps to get back into position during the pitch.*
Closed stance: *The foot closest to the pitcher is placed a tiny bit forward. This stance allows you to cover more of the plate with your bat. However,* ***turning your head to keep both eyes on the pitcher may be more of a strain****.*
If pointing your forward foot toward home plate proves to be uncomfortable, try adjusting it so that your toes point 45 degrees more toward the pitcher.

Discussion Questions
1. Which stance do you prefer? Why?
2. Which stance is most difficult for keeping your eyes on the pitcher?

2. Vocabulary

Natural Spoken Baseball English
The following items come from the speech of actual coaches, players, and other baseball specialists.

A. Cluster Challenge:
Complete the collocations using these words.
What's a collocation? A collocation is a combination of words in a language that happens very often and more frequently than would happen by chance.

slide/extension/front/stealer/path/tag/lead/cage/barrel/contact/tee/stride/backspin
*you may use one of these terms 3 times in one of the items below

1. What happens is we get backspin that comes off of **the** _____ and that's what gives the ball lift, length, and speed.
2. You don't have to try to kill every ball—80% will get you 100%. All it takes for you to do this is lineup, nice rhythm, and get **good** _____ . That's all you need.
3. So, now once we get the _____ **foot** going correctly and we load, stride, swing, now we work on the hands.
4. _____ , _____ , _____ ! Plenty of time. Make sure he catches it.
5. It had that **nice** _____ on it and that is the key to really hitting the ball with authority and hitting home runs.

6. I am going to put this ball on **the** _____ and I want you to start normal. I want you to do a weight shift, go back and then forward.
7. Uh, almost never. I try not to, I try not to _____ **head first**. I think, uh, there are too many things that can go wrong: break a hand, a wrist.
8. This is **the** _____ area. Uh, this is pretty much where I spend most of my day. If I am not at home or in class, I am either here or in the locker room and practice so, uh, this is where we hit as a team.
9. Always remember that our **swing** _____ is short to [the baseball] and long through [the baseball].
10. Wow, God, that looks like a **big** _____ ! Okay, so now he throws over. What is your first step?
11. To force the hands to come forward and to not drop the back shoulder and hands, we are going to do a drill called high _____ **toss** and it looks like this: I am simply going to toss it high into the strike zone and he is going to work on pulling his hands forward.
12. Um, what we're going to do in this drill is we're just going to take swings into a mat or into a pad and we're going to stop at our _____ **point** and check ourselves.
13. To be a **base** _____ , you want to take your lead off the back corner of the base. It's a crossover and two shuffle steps. That should put me right at the cut of the infield here.

B. Collocation Match-Up:

Match the two parts of these phrases.

1. ____ runner   a. bat
2. ____ drive   b. stolen
3. ____ hitter   c. hand-eye
4. ____ base   d. leg
5. ____ coordination e. batting
6. ____ speed   f. big league
7. ____ lift   g. home
8. ____ guy   h. base
9. ____ practice   i. gap
10. ____ run   j. line

CLUSTER CHALLENGE
Read numbers 1-13 (A.) again.

What other baseball collocations did you find in the above cluster challenges?

C. Skill Practice:
Complete each naturally spoken sentence using the given vocabulary terms below.

1. Yeah, you're going to get in a _____ at some point—all great hitters, no matter who you are, they have them every summer: from the Mike Trouts, the Albert Pujols, the Manny Ramirezs.
    a. hit b. short hop c. slump
2. We are looking for a short _____ . We are looking for a short swing from the shoulder to the ball. It is the most direct route. We look for the elbows to stay in a downward position.
    a. stride b. steal c. runner
3. _____ and overall technique are much more important to us [college coaches] during the hitting portion of our evaluations than how far you hit the ball. We'd rather see the hitters concentrate on just driving the ball, hitting line drives rather than getting long and trying to muscle up very often.
    a. bat head b. bat lag c. bat speed
4. Chris is going to demonstrate, we will get to our contact position and then he is going to try to extend along the _____ , the plain of the pitch, as long as he can, keeping this hand from rolling over as long as he can and then rolling over high on most pitches.
    a. efficient swing b. BP c. bat path
5. What happened to the orange _____ , did it go back in the bag? I have another one in my bag; we will find out what they did with it, but I have a yellow one in there, yeah? I know maybe it's over there but use the yellow one, Jeff.
    a. base b. cage c. donut
6. Now, what we want to do is, as the bat moves into contact position, we are going to have a slight weight shift forward to a _____ front leg and this is how it looks.
    a. loose b. special c. firm
7. See I think the craziest thing about Mike is that when gets in the box, his _____ , he has no _____ , he just starts moving around.
    a. strength b. rhythm c. hand-eye
8. All right, guys, so today's batting tip is on how to hit a baseball like Mike Trout. Now you know, a lot of expectations are going to be put on him this year because he's had a really successful year and his rookie season, and you know, when I look at his swing, some of the words that kind of come to mind are speed, quickness, strength, and _____ power.
    a. explosive b. average c. little

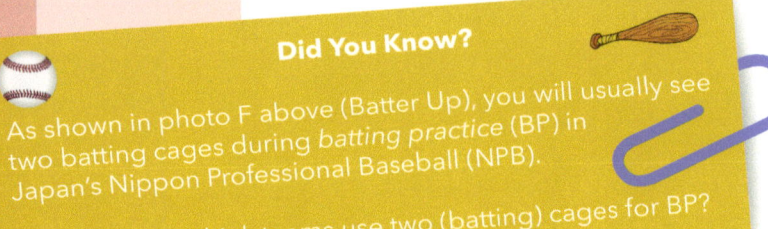

Did You Know?

As shown in photo F above (Batter Up), you will usually see two batting cages during *batting practice* (BP) in Japan's Nippon Professional Baseball (NPB).

1. Why do you think teams use two (batting) cages for BP?
2. Do you think this is a good idea?

3. Insider Baseball Talk:

You never go in a slump.
Let's go to the cage and watch former World Series Champion hitters Cecil Fielder (two-time Silver Slugger winner) and Wally Backman instruct a player on hitting.

A. Watch and Listen-In (Video 9)
Please go to
www.sportsEnglish.org/media

Optional: Focus on watching the video at least one time before completing the gap-filling exercise below.

B. Gap-Filling:
Watch the video and fill in the blanks with the vocabulary you hear.

Wally:	When you struggle, you try to _____ the ball harder…
Player:	Harder.
Wally:	and harder and _____ .
Player:	And it don't work.
Wally:	And you say, and you take that out of your mind and go, "You know what, I'm gonna lay down a couple of _____ down?'
Cecil:	You never go in a slump.
Wally:	Uh-uh, it'll stop you from _____ .
Wally:	The year I hit .320; you take 26 hits away from me (that's how many _____ _____ I had)…
Cecil:	Yeah.
Wally:	and [then] I probably hit .270.
Player:	Without a doubt.
Cecil:	_____ .
Wally:	You know?
Player:	Maybe even a little worse than that.
Wally:	You know, you only _____ do it once a day. Or show it once a day, at least! You know? So, you know?
Player:	Yeah.

C. Pair Work
1. Research and discuss any unfamiliar vocabulary from the video.
2. Discuss the meaning of these key baseball terms: *bunt hits, slump, slumping*.
3. Practice the conversation with a partner.

D. Discussion Questions
1. What do Wally and Cecil suggest will get a hitter out of a slump? Do you agree?
2. According to Wally, what helped him raise his batting average to .320 that one year in MLB?
3. How would Wally's batting average have decreased the year he hit .320?
4. What did Wally estimate his average would drop to?
5. According to Wally, how often does a player need to practice bunting?
6. Is bunting popular in your country's baseball culture? Why or why not?

E. Conversation Strategy
Go: Multi-Meaning Term

What does *go* mean when Wally said, "And you take that out of your mind and *go*, you know what, I'm gonna lay down a couple of **bunts** down?"

CHALLENGE
What are some baseball words that have more than one meaning?

"Go" Explained

"Go" is another way of saying what someone else says in a conversation. When using it in the third person, you can use "goes," ex. He goes, So, let's pitch Smith.

You probably know the more common form of "go," which means to move or travel: "I have to go to the bathroom." However, according to learnersdictionary.com, there are 27 meanings of "go" and all of its forms. "Go" and its forms are important to know, as it's a high-frequency word in English.

4. Insider Baseball Talk:
"Way to make him throw it!"

You just watched a video and read dialogue about hitting talk. Now let's go down to the field and watch Wally Backman coaching third base. Listen to him instruct the runner, Doc Brooks, on tagging up. Next, we hear Doc greeted by his coach near the dugout.

A. Photo Warm-Up
1. Describe each photo. Try to use complete sentences.
2. In photo A, what do you think the umpire, third base coach, runner, and third baseman are all looking at?
3. In photo B, what do you think is happening?

B. Watch and Listen-In (Video 10)
Please go to
www.sportsEnglish.org/media

Optional: Focus on watching the video at least one time before completing the gap-filling exercise below.

C. Gap-Filling:
Using terms from the words below, watch the video and fill in the blanks with the vocabulary you hear. **stuff/safe/tag**

> **Wally:** Tag, tag, tag, _____ ! Tag, Doc. Tag, Doc. Go for it! Go for it, Doc!
> **Umpire:** _____ !
> **Larry Olenberger, hitting coach:** Way to make him throw it right there. That's good _____ . That a baby!

D. Put the Terms From the Above Video Dialogue in the Correct Column

Instruction
- tag
- _____
- _____

Praise/Encouragement
- That's good stuff
- _____
- _____

E. Discussion Questions
1. Do you think Wally said *"Tag, tag, tag, tag"* too many times? Why or why not?
2. In the video, what does *"Go for it"* mean?
3. When Doc came back to the dugout, what happened?
4. How many different ways did the coach praise Doc when he returned to the dugout? What were the three praises?
5. In the video, the coach said, "Way to make him throw it right there." Who is *him*?

F. Practice
With a partner, read aloud the dialogue between Wally and Doc, and then between Coach Larry and Doc.

5. Graph Skills and Reading Spotlight

Bunting: A Lost Art? *In the 2019 season, five NPB clubs recorded over 100 sacrifice hits (SH).*

Did You Know?

Is bunting really dead (around the world)? Well, in Japan's top league, Nippon Professional Baseball (NPB), bunting is still alive and well. However, as you will learn at the end of this unit, when comparing international pro leagues, data indicates that in most leagues, sacrifice hits or bunts (SH) per plate appearances (PA) are generally down over the last five years. *As a matter of fact, during the 2020 season, two MLB clubs (the Brewers and Rays) had zero SH. Why?

1. Have you learned how to bunt? Why or why not?
2. In which part of the world do you think bunting will continue to increase or decrease? Why?

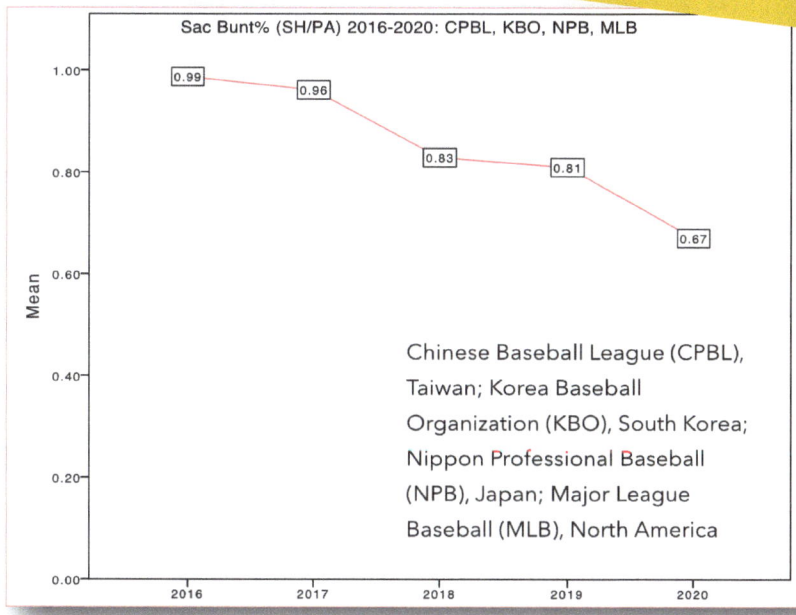

A. Warm-Up
1. What does this chart explain about sacrifice hits/bunts over the last five seasons across pro baseball in Asia and North America?
2. Based on this graph, which year does the sacrifice hit percentage per plate appearance (SH/PA) reach a low point?
3. Do you think the trend in this graph will change in the future? Explain your answer.

B. Key Vocabulary

Here are some terms related to the reading below.
Match the terms (1-6) with the definitions (a-f).

1. ___ league
2. ___ club
3. ___ bunting
4. ___ sacrifice hit (SH)
5. ___ statistic/stat
6. ___ category

a. to hit a baseball lightly with the bat so that the ball rolls for only a short distance
b. a group of things that are similar in some way
c. a sports team or organization
d. a group of sports teams that play against each other
e. a number representing a piece of information
f. a bunt that allows a runner to go to the next base while the batter is put out

C. Use the Terms from B (1-6) to Complete the Passage Below.
Make Sure to Use the Correct Form of the Term.

D. Read the Following Passage and Analyze the Graph

Is Bunting a Lost Art Everywhere?

According to data, the Central League (CL) Pacific League (PL) within Nippon Professional Baseball (NPB) perhaps stresses the importance of **1.**_____ more than MLB, KBO, and CPBL. In 2019, the Los Angeles Dodgers **2.**_____ _____ or bunts (SH) stood as the most for any MLB **3.**_____ (55), while NPB's top-ranked team in this category, Hiroshima Carp, had more than double what the Dodgers had, with 111 SH. Japan's NPB plays 143 games per season, 18 less than MLB (162), which makes this **4.**_____ even more impressive. Additionally, four other NPB clubs recorded over 100 SH in 2019. Also, in the 2019 statistical **5.**_____ of SH%, MLB's National League (NL) resulted in .57 compared to 1.75 SH/PA in NPB's Central League (CL); this represents a significant difference. Both NL and PL do not have the DH rule, where the pitchers hit in those **6.**_____ . For more analysis of SH/PA from international pro baseball leagues, see the diagram on the next page.

Note: American League (AL) in MLB; Central League (CL) in NPB, Japan; Chinese Baseball League (CPBL), Taiwan; Korea Baseball Organization (KBO), South Korea; National League (NL) in MLB; Pacific League (PL) in NPB, Japan

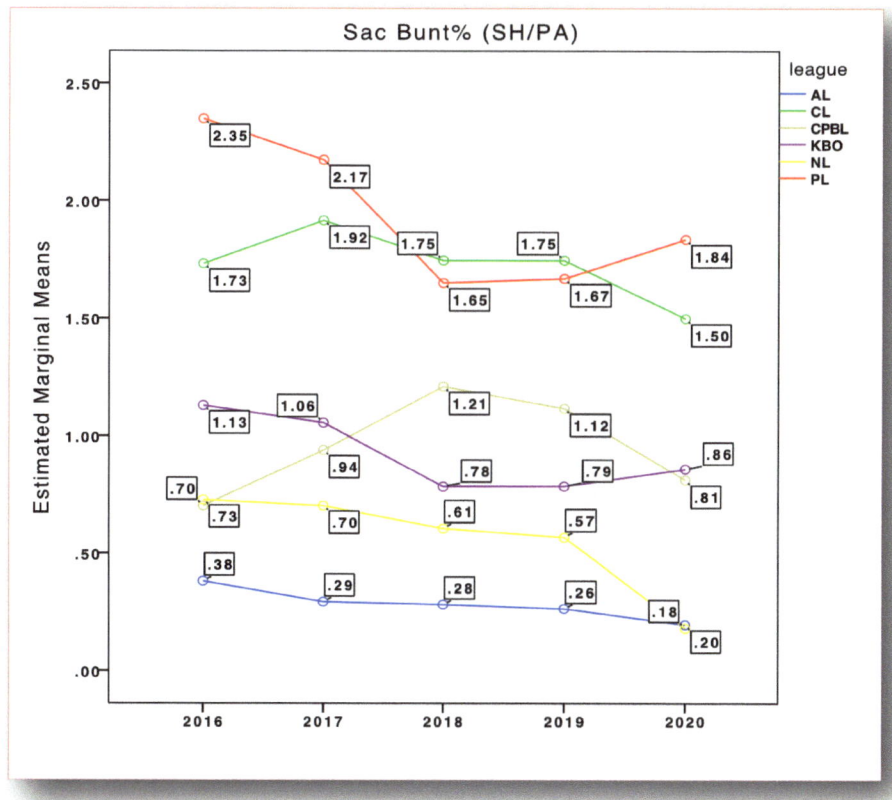

Talk TIME

E. Answer the Following Questions.
Then Discuss Your Answers in a Group.

1. Which league had the highest sac bunts/hits% over the last five years? Which had the lowest? What were the numbers?
2. In which leagues does this chart suggest that bunting (part of the small ball approach) is used most and least?
3. Why do we see a decline in sacrifice bunts over recent years?
4. Do you want to see bunting increasing or decreasing? Why?

F. Agree or Disagree
Do you agree with the following statements?
Discuss with a partner.

Agree or Disagree

1. Practicing the bunt every day is good.
2. The game has changed and bunting will occur less and less.
3. Everyone should be required to practice bunting.
4. Small ball is the best way to generate runs.

UNIT 6
Scouting: Describing And Evaluating Players

Topics: Describing players, Sal's important questions, Scout's job, The Scouting report, Skills in each position

1. Batter Up! Vocabulary

A. Who are the players or prospects?
Match the descriptions from scouting reports (1-4) to the players (A-D).

B. Talkin' Photos
Discuss the photos. Try speaking in complete sentences

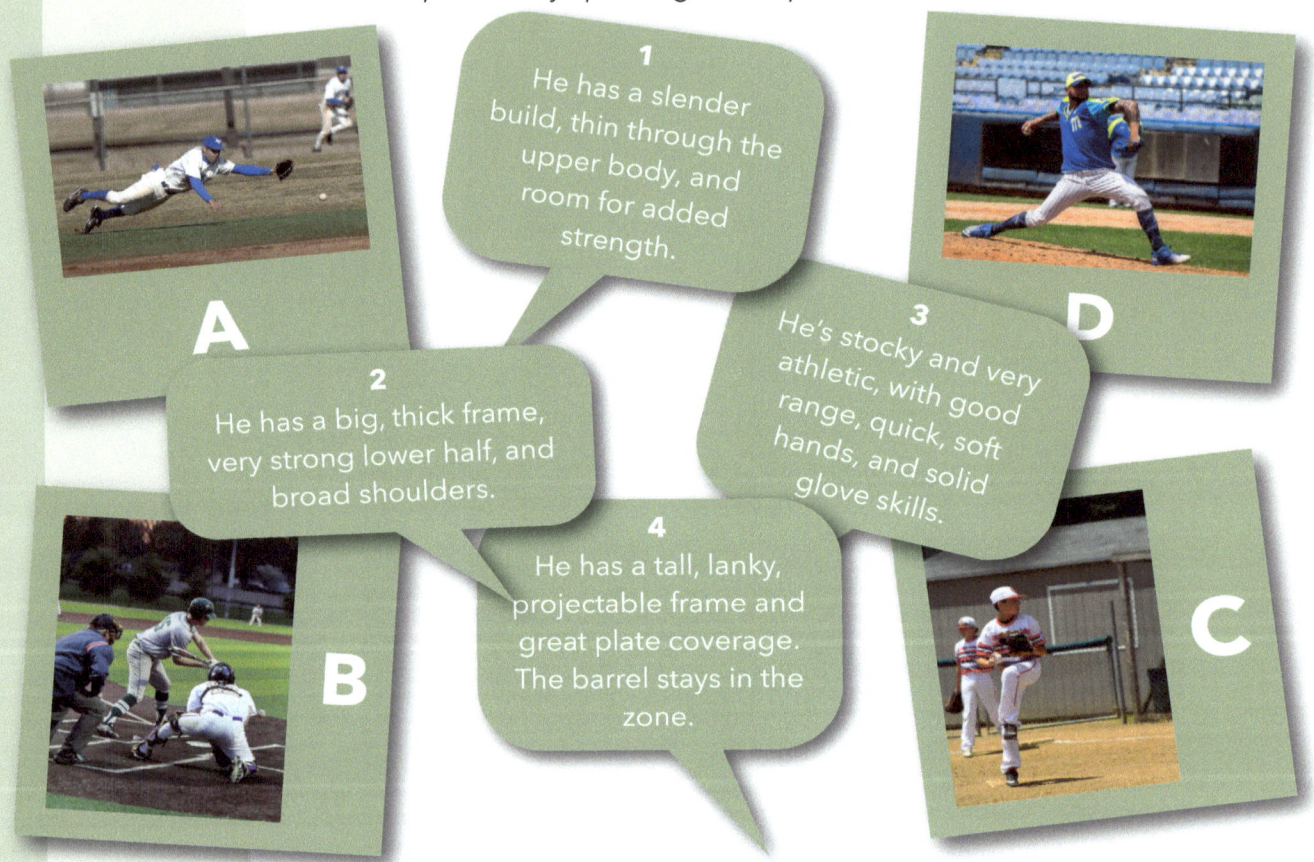

1. He has a slender build, thin through the upper body, and room for added strength.

2. He has a big, thick frame, very strong lower half, and broad shoulders.

3. He's stocky and very athletic, with good range, quick, soft hands, and solid glove skills.

4. He has a tall, lanky, projectable frame and great plate coverage. The barrel stays in the zone.

B. These words and phrases are used to describe physical appearance.
Match the opposites.

1. lanky	2. stocky	3. strong	4. projectable frame
a. thin	b. short	c. unlikely growth	d. weak

C. These words are used to describe a player's skills.
Match the words that have similar meanings.

1. athleticism	2. speed	3. tools	4. power	5. quick
a. skillset	b. able-bodied	c. strength	d. fast	e. velo/velocity

E. Scouting Duties

Scouts have many job *responsibilities* and rely on *tools* to help them evaluate or grade players.

Put the term in the correct box.

evaluate (v)	computer	hold workouts	attend showcases
notepad	video camera	sign (v)	scout (v)
tablet	stopwatch	identify prospects	grade (v)
speed/radar gun	write reports		

Responsibilities	Tools for evaluation

2. Grades

As mentioned above, an important part of a scouting report is OFP. To judge OFP, there are other grades to consider first.

Insider Term

Overall future potential or ***OFP*** is a grade you assign to a prospect based on a scale your club uses—just like how a teacher gives a student a grade. Nowadays, many MLB scouts use the 20-80 scale. This is where the scout projects or predicts how the player will grade or play upon developing. This projection is based on comparable players and the players' skills, makeup, family genetics, and history—all parts of the equation for ***OFP***. Don't forget ***OFP***!

OFP (Overall Grades)

GRADE	CLASS
66-80	Major League Star
50-65	Solid, Everyday Regular
40-49	Bench/Below Average Regular
30-39	Organizational Guy

Source: FanGraphs

Hitting Grades

GRADE	HOME RUNS	AVERAGE
80	38+	.320+
70	30 to 38	.305 to .319
60	22 to 29	.290 to .304
50	16 to 21	.265 to .289
40	10 to 15	.245 to .264
30	5 to 9	.225 to .244
20	0 to 4	.199 to .224

Player's Grades

TOOL	NOW	FUTURE
Hitting	40	60
Power	20	35
Speed	60	65
Fielding	55	60
Throwing	35	50
OFP		54
*Adj OFP		56

adjusted OFP *In many cases, adjusted OFP is created automatically (within a computer application/program) based on the player's position, tool grades, and age. For example, because first base is a power position, a solid hitting yet powerless first baseman who is older will likely have a much lower adjusted OFP than a right-fielder with the same tool grades but who is younger.*

After completing these grades, the scout will write a summary about the player's strengths, weaknesses, and potential.

A. True (T) or False (F).
Write T or F for the following statements. If F, correct the statement.   *True or False*

1. The scout put an OFP on this player that projects a Major League Star.
2. The scout graded this player as now having below-average power.
3. The scout feels that in the future, the player could hit over .300.
4. The scout felt that fielding was this player's best tool.

3. Sal's Important Questions

Sal Agostinelli (left) during the signing of pitcher Erubiel Armenta (R). Mexico, 2019

"Scout everyone!"

Sal Agostinelli works as International Scouting Director for the Philadelphia Phillies. After his professional playing career ended, he began scouting and has signed players for over 30 years. In 2018, Agostinelli was honored by Major League Baseball, receiving the prestigious Scout of the Year award. He has been involved in finding and signing big names like All-Star catcher Carlos Ruiz and current Miami Marlins top-line starting pitcher Sixto Sanchez. A young, new scout once asked Sal if he needed to scout only the targeted star player at a particular game. Sal replied, "Scout everyone!" That kind of scouting approach has led to Sal's team signing players whom other clubs overlooked, leaving no stone unturned.

When writing a scouting report or talking about a player, Sal always wants to know the answers to these important questions:

- What does the player look like (physically)?
- What's the player like (makeup)?
- What skills does the player have?
- Where do you see them in your future projection, ex. starter, reliever (OFP)?

A. As a scout, you will write a scouting report.

The boxes below contain **Sal's Important Questions**, which you'll need to answer in a scouting report. Put the descriptions in the box with the correct questions.

She's/He's 17 years old, lanky: 6'1, 160 pounds. • She/He has great makeup, high baseball IQ. • She's/He's a 60 OFP. She/He has leadership qualities. • She's/He's a hard worker. • She/He has excellent arm speed and velocity. • They project as a frontline MLB starter. • She/He has a projectable build/frame. • She/He has a 4-seam fastball that touches 94 miles per hour (mph) and an above-average changeup—sits 81. • She's/He's a high draft choice.

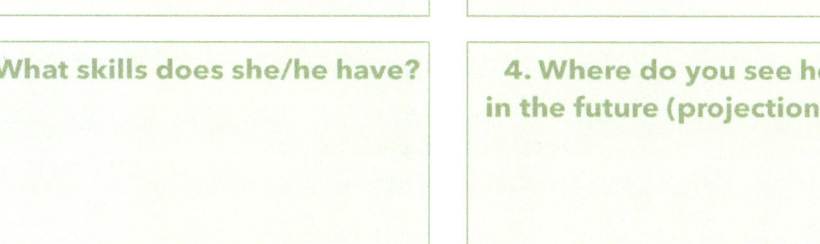

1. What does she/he look like?	2. What's the player like?

3. What skills does she/he have?	4. Where do you see her/him in the future (projection)? OFP?

4. Insider Baseball Talk:
He's got a Major League arm, no question!

Photo Warm-Up
1. What is their job?
2. What device is in their hands?

65

Let's listen to Wally's scouting reports on Dumas Garcia and Steve Garrabrants.

A. Watch and Listen-In (Video 11)
Please go to www.sportsEnglish.org/media
Optional: Focus on watching the video at least one time before completing the exercise below.

B. Watch and Listen to Wally's Scouting Reports.
Complete the table.

	Dumas Garcia	Steve Garrabrants
Position	_____	_____
Best tool(s)?	Got an exceptional arm _____ .	_____ out as good as anybody. He's got speed. He's developed _____ .
Why sign this player?	He's got big league _____ . There's no question.	He was a little smaller; he's gotten bigger and _____ .
Projection/Profile	How he _____ now in the levels that he goes to is really going to be interesting. He's got a major league _____ , no question.	Major league _____ player because he can play so many positions.

Everyday English SHE'S/HE'S/THEY GOT

- Notice that Wally used **he's got** when describing the skills a player *possesses* or has.
- She's/He's got is *informal*, like much of Baseball English.
  ex. **She's/He's got** a loose arm.

- **She's/He's got** is short for **She/He has got**.
  ex. **She/He has got** a loose arm.

- Someone in scouting may ask, "**Watcha** got on him?" "**Watcha**" is slang and a shortened, faster way of saying "*What do you?*"
  This means, what are your thoughts or opinions on this player or what OFP grade do you have on them?
  An example answer is, "*I got a 50 [grade] on 'em.*"

- Someone might also ask, "*What's she/he got?*"
  She's/He's got a plus slider.

Practice
C. What Scouts Got on Players?
Complete the sentences from scouting talk.
What's she/he got?

funky   trophies   velocity   pop

1. He's got kind of a _____ delivery. He is over the top and he has got a good arm so we are going to see fastballs down in the zone, below the belt.
2. At the plate, she's got some _____ . She's good.
3. He's got _____ , this kid. He hit 96 [mph] on the gun.
4. She has won a lot of stuff. She's got some _____ .

D. Pair Work
1. Research and discuss any unfamiliar vocabulary from the video.
2. Practice reading Wally's scouting reports with a partner.
3. Using the Internet, report what happened to these two players after they played for the South Georgia Peanuts. Did they make it to the big leagues (MLB)? Which level did they reach?

Hint: Check *www.baseball-reference.com*

E. Group or Pair Discussion
1. What are the pros and cons of the players (Garcia and Garrabrants) described in the video?
2. Imagine you work as a scouting director for a pro baseball club. Based on the pros and cons you wrote above, which player do you recommend the general manager sign? Why?

5. Scouting Reports

Scouting Report Grades: The 2-8 Scale
According to Scouting and Scoring, MLB scouts began grading players from 2 to 8 for each skill—a whole number between 2 (weak) and 8 (superior). This was an attempt to make the process of grading more uniform and objective or fair by measuring players' abilities on a similar scale or instrument. Scouts were asked to assign a grade to each player's performance for skill categories for position players (fielding, running, power, etc.) and for pitchers (fastball, curve, slider, control, command, etc.).

Insider Info: The Bureau

The former Major League Scouting Bureau (MLSB), like MLB clubs, scouted amateur prospects and wrote reports to which MLB clubs had access. In 2018, the bureau stopped evaluating players, but it still provides video and medical information on players to MLB clubs. Today, you can find the bureau's scouting reports through the National Baseball Hall of Fame's website: collection.baseballhall.org/PASTIME/scouting-reports If you want to see MLB scouting reports, check these out!

What can a future scout learn from reading these reports?

A. Reading Challenge: Prospect Report
Below, read the bureau's report on a young Matt Harvey.

MLSB Follow Report Harvey, Matt E

School/Team:	R E Fitch Senior HS, Groton, CT	Position: RHS	
Sch/Tm Type:	HS	Adjusted OFP:	65
Academic Class:	HS	Basic OFP:	65
Grad Date:	06/2007	Adjusted OFP:	
Draft Eligible Year:	2007		
Born:	03/27/1989	Report Date:	04/10/2007
Height:	6' 04"	Games:	1
Weight:	210	Innings:	4
Bats:	Right	Scout:	Short, P
Throws:	Right		
Comments:			
Home Address	School Address		
Notes			
	Biopter: Yes	Psych Test:	No
	Medicals: No	HHQ:	No
	Filmed: No	Eyewear:	None
Home Phone:	School Phone:		
Cell Phone:			
HS Graduation:	06/2007		
Habits:	Good	Agility: Good	Phys Maturity: Good
Letter of Intent:	UNC Chapel Hill, Chapel Hill, NC		
Dedication:	Good	Aptitude: Good	Emot Maturity: Good
Arm Action:	Excel	Delivery: Good	Camp/Tournament:
Wind-up:	Semi	Windup Arm Angle: H3/4	Summer Club:
School Next Year:	UNC Chapel Hill, Chapel Hill, NC		

Category	Present	Future	Velocity	Comments
Fast Ball	6	7	90-94	Most 91-92. Several 94's 1st inn. More in the tank.
FB Movement	5	5		Best mvmnt & life downstairs.
Curve	4	6	72-77	Late & hard, str down break on higher vel ones.
Slider	0	0	0-0	Cutter in last eval, abil to dev into usable SL. None today.
None	0	0	0-0	
Change	4	5	81-83	In dev stage. Keeps arm spd & slot. Will improve w/ use.
Control	4	6		Around plate. Occ loc FB.
Poise	5	6		Focused. Does not rattle.
Baseball Instinct	6	6		Def feel for mound. Knows when not right, abil to adjust.
Aggressiveness	6	6		No fear, not afraid to get in kitchen.

Physical Description: Ideal young pitcher's build. Added 20 good lbs since last yr. More growth pot. Pot Joe Nathan type build. Simple, basic mech. Ext both ends. No glaring flaws.
Injury/Medical Update: Groin pull last week. Blister on RT index finger recently. Both fine now. Signed to UNC Chapel Hill. Scott Boros advisor. Father, Ed, is Matt's HS coach.
Abilities: Clean as a whistle, gifted arm. Ball jumps from hand with case. Enuf 93-94 FB's to proj futr well above avg. Late life down, occ bore, tight to RHH. Flashes nasty hammer CB, pot out pitch. Ath.
Weaknesses: FB above belt often str. Primarily up in zone today, have seen much better dwnhl in past. Feel for seldom used CIR CHG. Inconsistent CB, some tight & right, some loose & up.
Summation: Still early, today only 2nd time out. Predetermined 65 pitch assignment. Premium prospect. All the makings of a frontline of ML rot starter. Looking forward to UNC, but believe signable at top dollar.

Major League Scouting Bureau's 2007 report on Matt Harvey.
Archives, National Baseball Hall of Fame

Key: excel/excellent; H/high; FB/fastball; mvmt/movement; enuf/enough; pot/potential; ext/extends; RT/right; occ/occasional; str/straight; dwnhl/downhill; proj/project; futr/future; avg/average; ML/Major League; CIR CHG/circle change; rot/rotation; w/with

B. Discussion Questions
1. Notice that the scout wrote many abbreviations in the report and even misspelled words. Why do you think the scout did that?
2. What's the most difficult part about reading this report?
3. What OFP does the scout have on Harvey?
4. According to the scout's pitching grades, what's Harvey's best pitch, present and future?
5. Which pitches need the most improvement?
6. What is the most impressive thing about this player?
7. Did Matt Harvey reach the expectations of this scout as described in the summation?
8. What did the scout mean about the players when he wrote "No fear, not afraid to get in kitchen"?

6. Report: Putting It All Together

A. From what you have learned so far in this unit
Write three short descriptions of famous players. Include their *names*, *physical appearances*, and *best skills*. Congratulations! You are on your way to writing scouting reports!

What is the name of the player? What does he look like (physical appearance)?	What are the player's skills?
What is the name of the player? What does he look like (physical appearance)?	What are the player's skills?
What is the name of the player? What does he look like (physical appearance)?	What are the player's skills?

B. Role Play: Scouting Discussion
Walk around and ask classmates about a player they chose to describe. Then write down what they said below.
Ask:

	1	2	3
What's the player's name?			

What do you got on 'em?

	1	2	3
1. What does he/she look like?			
2. What are the player's skills?			

7. Choose Your Weapon: Stalker II or Smart Coach

Did You Know?
Inside a Scout's Toolbox

As a scout, you will need to evaluate the speed or velocity at which a pitcher throws and also the exit velocity that comes off a hitter's bat. You can measure speed with more expensive radar/speed guns such as *Stalker II*, used by many MLB scouts, OR you can find a less expensive speed measuring device that fits in your pocket, called Smart Coach. As explained in a YouTube video by former MLB player Doug Bernier, both have both pros and cons.

Doug Bernier,
www.probaseballinsider.com
YouTube Channel: Pro Baseball Insider

A. Figure It Out
As mentioned, a pocket radar device such as Smart Coach and a larger professional radar gun such as *Stalker II* (both pictured above) have both PROS or advantages, and CONS or disadvantages. Look at these other PROS and CONS about Smart Coach on the next page and sort them into the right category. Also, think about some other PROS and CONS for *Smart Coach* besides the ones listed on the next page.

- Price: A professional radar gun is about $1200 US; Smart Coach (pocket radar) is $399 US. • Smart Coach is made of plastic; Pro Stalker II is made of strong aluminum. • Simple: easy to operate • Versatile: works in front or behind the baseball • Battery life won't last on <u>continuous mode</u> throughout a game

PROS (advantages)	CONS (disadvantages)

B. Workaround
How can you solve or fix the battery problem with Smart Coach (pocket radar)?

C. Agree or Disagree
Do you agree with the following statements? Discuss with a partner (if possible).

Agree or Disagree

1. Stalker II is more durable than *Pocket Radar*.
2. I prefer using *Pocket Radar* over *Stalker II*.
3. A speed gun or radar gun is necessary for scouts.
4. It is worth paying more for *Stalker II* than the less expensive *Pocket Radar*.

Which device would you buy—Stalker II or Pocket Radar? Why?

8. Reading Spotlight: Meet Manabu Kuramochi

A. Pre-Reading Warm-Up
1. What is *TrackMan* used for in baseball?
2. What job do you want in baseball?

B. Vocabulary
1. Complete the blank lines in the reading, using the key vocabulary terms from the word cloud below.

PROFILE
Experience: Front Office Executive, Coach, and Professional Baseball Player
Date of Birth: October 21, 1978
Pace of Birth: Tokyo, Japan
Position: Second Baseman and Center Fielder

analysts   analytics   favorite   job   tryout
attaboy   baseball   player   attaboy
wow   dad   indy ball

C. Read
Optional: Try reading aloud with a partner. Take turns reading after a sentence or two.

The Long Road to International Scouting Director

"Zero" English
So, did you speak English when you arrived to play baseball in the U.S.?
Zero.
Wow!
I mean, I just played 1._____. I learned. I never studied anything.
So, you went to college and played in Japan?
Yeah, [as a matter of fact] I played on a club team in junior high school, the same one as Daisuke Matsuzaka.

Undrafted
So, why did you go to the States?
I didn't get drafted in Japan (NPB), so I decided to go to the States to be a pro.
Where did you play?
2._____, it's called Southeastern League. That was 2002 or 2003, the brand new league.

"I Went to 27 Tryouts"
Can you talk about the process of getting on an indy ball team?
A friend told me about tryouts. Before I left Japan, I just told my friend, "Okay. I'm coming for the 3._____." And then I went there. I couldn't make any teams. I went to like three, four tryouts. I couldn't make it. So, I went to 27 tryouts in the States over two months. 4._____.
You really wanted it.
Yeah. February to April. Finally, number 28, I made it.
That's a great story. You had determination.

Learning English to Survive
So, how did you learn English?
In spring training, no Japanese, only American people, Samoans, Dominicans. And then the terrible thing was we stayed in a motel—one room, two beds, four guys.
Oh, man. You had to sleep on the bed with somebody. Yeah. So, I had to communicate with them and I tried to learn English.
Did you get a book or did you take lessons?
I had nothing. I didn't have anything.
So, you've learned all the English you had through your job?
Yes.

The Tough Journey
Where did you play pro baseball?
Pensacola, Florida; Calgary, Canada; in Germany, where I coached and played.
Wow. I didn't know you lived in Germany. Did you like the food over there? I liked it, but I didn't always like being in Europe, because being Asian is tough to live there. They kicked me out of their restaurant. I went there with a teammate.
Huh?
The guy from the restaurant kicked me out.
Why? Because I'm Asian.
Oh, that's terrible. I'm sorry that happened to you.
A couple of times it happened. So, I decided to leave and went back to Calgary for two years.
So, how many years outside Japan in baseball?
Six years.

Working in the Front Office
Can you tell us a little bit about your job in baseball now?
I just got promoted to international director of scouting for Chiba Lotte Marines in Japan. Until last year, I worked as a scout, all over the world.
And now you have more responsibility?
Yeah. I decide who we're going to sign and also cross-checking.
That's an interesting job. Do you use analytics and how do you feel about analytics?
I used to work for TrackMan—I think it's useful to make a decision. I don't have to make a decision by myself. Also, 5._____ push me to sign players as well. So, it makes it easier to decide on a 6._____ who we should sign. But not only analytics, I think. We need to scout. We have to find out what's happening in the stadium, how players act, make up, all these things. So, I will say 50% (7._____)-50% (scouting) will be great for scouting. But sometimes I have to fight with the analysts. That's a tough part of my 8._____ as well.
What's the most enjoyable part of your job?
I signed Leonys Martin last year—second game, he had a home run. I was so happy. If I sign someone and they're successful, that's good for me. I'm like a 9._____ for them. You have feelings like that.

Putting English to Work
How do you use English in your job?
Negotiating with agents and taking care of foreign players during the season.
And you speak with the players a lot during the season, who you sign?
Yes. I have to take care of the players a lot; they always have a problem.

"My Rule"
Before COVID hit, did you usually travel overseas and see players you want to sign in person?
This is my rule—if I don't see them play, I'm not going to sign.
Okay. But now due to COVID you kind of have to rely on video scouting?
Yes.

Getting In
What advice do you have to people who want to get a job in baseball?
It's all about connections. It depends on who you know. And you have to show them what you know in baseball, what's your specialty. I was with the Kansas City Royals, and for the first four years, I didn't get any money. I worked for them for free—I had to prove my ability.

Choice Word
What's one of your favorite baseball terms?
The first time I went to play in the U.S. people were saying, "10._____." I had no idea. I had no idea what they're saying. "What is that?" Probably that is my 11._____ because it's the first word I learned in baseball. I had no idea. I asked the teammate, "What is attaboy?"

Manabu also worked as an MLB scout and coached for various U.S. teams, including the Long Beach Armada of the Arizona Winter League.

D. Are the Sentences True (T) or False (F)? If False (F), Correct the Sentence.

True or False

1. Manabu knew some English upon moving to the U.S.
2. Manabu came to the U.S. after he went undrafted in Japan.
3. Manabu made an indy ball team on his first tryout.
4. Manabu did not face any problems while playing and coaching.
5. Now, Manabu has a lot of responsibility in his job and has to deal with many problems sometimes.
6. To get a job in baseball, you only need knowledge.

E. Discussion Questions
1. How many different jobs has Manabu had in baseball? Which of these jobs do you want to do most, and why?
2. What is Manabu's rule for signing players? Do you agree with it? Why?
3. Have you faced discrimination like Manabu did when he had to leave the restaurant in Germany? Could you explain what happened to you?
4. What's your favorite baseball term? Why?

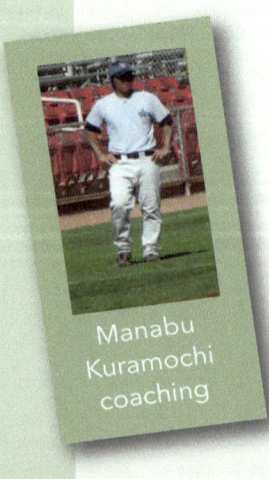
Manabu Kuramochi coaching

UNIT 7
Now Hiring: The Many Jobs In Baseball

Topics: Baseball jobs, Job skills, Front office, Job postings, Pioneering GM signs Trailblazers

1. Batter Up! Vocabulary

A. Match the photos to the terms below

A

B

C

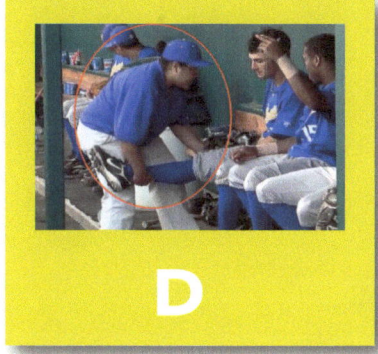
D

E

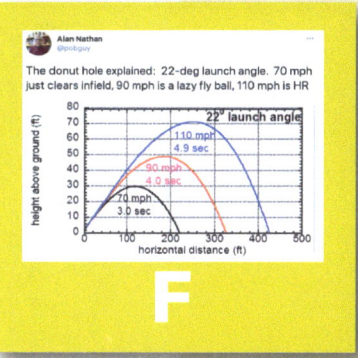
F

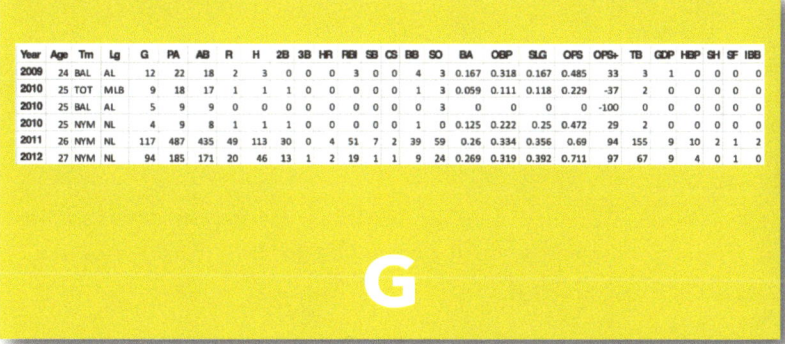
G

H

1. ___ reporter
2. ___ grounds crew
3. ___ bullpen catcher
4. ___ stats/statistics
5. ___ analytics/advanced metrics
6. ___ clubbie
7. ___ general manager/GM
8. ___ trainer

75

B. Match Each job to the Related Skills

1. ___ reporter
2. ___ grounds crew
3. ___ analytics associate
4. ___ clubbie
5. ___ general manager/GM
6. ___ trainer

a. player personnel, leadership, negotiating
b. knowledge of human anatomy
c. ability to cater to many people's needs, logistics, and planning
d. excellent writing and speaking skills
e. knowledge and experience in sports turf and baseball maintenance
f. research, understanding of statistics, computer coding, and programming skills

C. Which Box Does the Job Fit Into?

Throughout this book, you have learned that many jobs are related to the sport of baseball. These jobs can be team-related or involve working for other companies.
From the vocabulary above (in part A), put the term into the correct box.

Media	Data-Related	Front Office/ Baseball Operations	Team Support Staff	Stadium Operations

D. Words in Context: Concordance

Cluster Challenge: *Complete the collocations using these words in context: bullpen/stats/clubbie/fantasy/crew/reporter/analytics/assistant*

1. PITCHf/x, HITf/x, and TrackMan are technologies used for tracking the baseball used by an _____ department.
2. Longtime baseball _____ John Manuel wrote for Baseball America.
3. When he first got to the Blue Jays, he went from _____ catcher to first base coach.
4. If we know from the _____ that the pitcher can swing it, we'll treat him just like a normal hitter but generally we will just throw fastballs to each side of the plate to the pitcher, just try to get him to hit a little floater somewhere.
5. _____ managers and baseball fans are always trying to figure out what exactly players with injuries are going through. When can we expect them back on the field?
6. MLB must reimburse the minor league team $16,176 to pay the _____ for their in-season job.
7. Every inning, you see a guy come out and he is going to fix the mound every single inning. We are kind of like our own grounds _____.
8. The Houston Astros announced _____ general manager Brandon Taubman was fired for an outburst at female reporters after the Astros won the ALCS.

Role Play: Interpreter

1. Interpret these frequently used phrases in baseball from English to your language.

English ➡ Your first language or another language

1. We are going to talk about **some pitching**.
_____
_____

2. I'm going to show you **the slider**.
_____
_____

3. *You know what I mean?*
_____
_____

* The **bold** words can be replaced by other terms, ex. *I'm going to show you **the splitter**.*

2. Practice interpreting the above statements to a partner in their first language.

3. Replace the underlined words with other terms and practice saying those phrases.
   a. We are going to talk about _____.
   b. I'm going to show you _____.

3. Insider Baseball Talk:

I just got a call from Kevin.
Pre-Video Discussion: What are some jobs in the front office?

A. Vocabulary:
Match Each Term With Its Synonym
1. ___ uh-huh   a. pal
2. ___ officially   b. belongings
3. ___ buddy   c. Oh, no
4. ___ picked up   d. chosen
5. ___ property   e. formerly
6. ___ goddamn it   f. okay

Let's go into the dugout and watch Wally receive news from the front office about one of his players.

B. Watch and Listen-in (Video 12)
Please go to www.sportsEnglish.org/media
Optional: Focus on watching the video at least one time before completing the exercise below.

C. Gap-Filling:
Watch the video and fill in the blanks with the vocabulary you hear.

Part 1
Front office staff: Wally?
Wally: Yeah.
Front office staff: I just got a call from Kevin.
Wally: _____.
Front office staff: Jared Sutton is _____ of the Milwaukee Brewers.
Wally: Okay. Alright. Thank you.
Wally: _____!
Front office staff: Hey, Wally?
Wally: What?
Front office staff: Are you gonna tell him or do you want us to do something on the field?
Wally: No, no, no. Let me tell him first. Let me tell him.

Part 2
Wally: Where's Sutton?
Wally: Congratulations, the Milwaukee Brewers just _____.
Jared Sutton: Really?
Wally: Yep.
Jared Sutton: Cool.
Wally: Congratulations _____, it's good for you.
Jared Sutton: Appreciate it.
Wally: Get your _____ and get out of here!

D. Write T for True and F for False. If (F) False, Correct the Statement.

True or False

1. The front office informed Wally that Jared Sutton got picked up by another team.
2. Wally said, "Goddamn it!" because he felt upset about the news from the front office.
3. Jared Sutton got picked up by the Boston Red Sox.
4. The front office will inform Jared of this good news.
5. Jared seems pleased about the news that Wally gives him.

E. Discussion Questions
1. Why did the man from the front office need to speak with Wally in the middle of a game?
2. What does it mean that Jared is now property of another team?
3. Who will tell Jared about getting signed by Milwaukee: the front office or Wally? Do you agree with this?

To watch more of this scene and find out what level Jared will go to next, check out episode 4 of "Playing for Peanuts"–available for rent or purchase on Amazon and Vimeo.

4. Everyday English: Why Don't You…?

A team trainer helps players with injuries.

Warm-Up
1. What are some baseball injuries?
2. Do you think using *why don't you* or *you should* is more polite when giving someone a suggestion?

    Examples:
Why don't you try the pizza?
You should try the pizza.

A. Vocabulary:
Match Each Term With Its Opposite
1. uh-huh   2. ice   3. ahead
a. heat   b. disagree   c. behind

Let's go into the dugout to watch and listen as Wally speaks with Eldora Grandison, team trainer, about helping an injured player.

B. Watch and Listen-In (Video 13)
Go to www.sportsEnglish.org/media
Listen to the conversation and complete the sentences.

Wally: Why don't you, uh, go _____ and take him in and get some ice on im.
Eldora: I got _____ out here.
Wally: Oh, you do? Okay. Okay.
Eldora: _____ .

> **CONVERSATION STRATEGY**
>
> *Why don't you...*
> Notice how Wally used **Why don't you** when asking the trainer to ice the player's injury.
>
> - **Why don't you** is used for making a suggestion, as you see in the video.

C. Try It
Write two suggestions, using *Why don't you* as a starter.
1. _____
2. _____

D. Practice
Read your *Why don't you* suggestions to a partner. Your partner can respond with *uh-huh, okay, alright, got it*.

Or, if they do not agree with the suggestion, try a polite way of disagreeing, ex. *I'm good, no thanks, no thank you*, etc.

5. People in Baseball: Ups and Downs!

A. Vocabulary.
These terms are used to describe people's jobs in baseball.

1. Match the words that have similar meanings.

| 1. nerd | 2. camaraderie | 3. veneer | 4. introvert | 5. recover |
| a. mask | b. loner | c. geek | d. bounce back | e. friendship |

2. Complete the sentences in the reading using these key vocabulary terms:

- ballgame
- baseball
- challenge
- coaching
- camaraderie
- recover
- gratifying
- introvert
- nerd
- negotiating
- sightseeing
- veneer

B. Match the Descriptions (1-7) to the Job (A-G)

Noboru Katsuragawa
International Affairs
(Chunichi Dragons)
A

Chaewoo Lim
Senior Manager Baseball Operations
(Lotte Giants)
B

Jeeho Yoo
Journalist (Yonhap News)
C

David Kim
Pacific Rim Scout
(Minnesota Twins)

D

Brandon Knight
Pitching Coach
(SSG Landers)

E

Mike "Nino" Ninivaggi
High School Coach, Warrior Sports Camp Owner
(Wantagh High School)

F

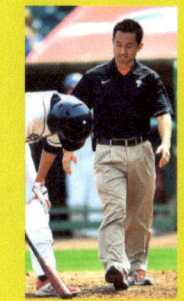

Taka Sakurai
Trainer
(Chiba Lotte Marines)

G

1. The most enjoyable part of my job is easily seeing the smile on a players face, whether it be a 9-year-old or a 35-year-old, when we've been working on something and it clicks and starts working. It's 1._____ to know that I might have helped that person advance and improve.

The most challenging part is the stress of knowing that I have no control over the performance of guys I've coached. I have to trust that I've done everything I can to help them and hope for the best. It's a bit like parenting and it's nerve wracking. The other bad part of the job: way too little time with family.

2. The best part of my job is getting to stay with the players and the team. If the players do well and the team wins, it's more enjoyable. Staying on the bench and being there with players is enjoyable.

The most challenging parts of my job are looking for foreign players abroad in the Dominican Republic, and Cuba. 2._____ with the Cuban Federation and also, interpreting English is a big challenge. For me, English is the biggest challenge because Spanish is my second language after Japanese.

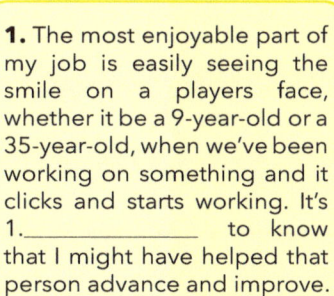

3. It's great luck to have your favorite job as work. The most enjoyable part of this job is that I can be directly involved in strategic planning. If you have this job, you can adjust the rosters and trade players in reality, not in video games. What else is more wonderful than this?

In Korea, there are only 10 professional 3._____ teams across the country. It means that there are few jobs in this field and it's very competitive. Also, MLB and NPB are in a similar situation. For this job, you might say goodbye to something like family, friends, town and even country; so did I. Nevertheless, if you still want this job, try it. Instead of missing a few pleasures for 4._____ you will enjoy baseball that no one else can taste.

4. My favorite part of the job is writing. I am such a 5._____ with words. I always enjoy crafting stories from games that I watch and people that I meet. That's honestly my favorite part and I can't imagine doing anything else for a living. In pre-pandemic times, I also enjoyed the traveling part of the job, seeing different parts of the world (though it's mostly hotel and stadiums and media centers, with little time left for actual 6._____).

For job challenges, it's a personal thing and not everyone has the same problem. I am an 7._____ by nature and early on in my career, it was hard for me to meet new people or cold call strangers. I've gotten better at it over time. Phone calls can still be a bit of a 8._____ but meeting new people is more fun now.

81

5. The most enjoyable part of my job is being able to teach young baseball players the best game ever invented. But more importantly, over the 38 years of 9._____ I've been able to build life-long relationships with our players, watching them grow as baseball players, but more importantly as wonderful human beings. Many have moved on to become educators and coaches themselves. Attending their weddings or something as simple as just having a nice dinner and catching up with them is what's been my favorite part of coaching.

The most challenging part of coaching high school baseball is dealing with the constant turnover of players every year. Creating a culture in your program is the first thing necessary to become successful. Hopefully, the players develop baseball skills and team 10._____ skills that perpetuate through the teams that follow. You need your teams to understand the importance of tradition and the responsibility of being part of a team that has a great tradition. It's being responsible for their actions on and off of the field.

6. The most enjoyable part of my job is knowing I have the ability to give a player the choice to pursue his dream of playing in MLB.

The most challenging part of my job is determining the intangibles. Another challenge is sifting through the players that truly have a desire and goal to play at the ML level and weeding out the ones that are 11._____ .

7. I'm not a player, but I can share those moments with them. I feel that's pretty cool. Not always easy but being happy and sorry with them as a team is pretty enjoyable.

I have to keep up with the players in my job. That's pretty challenging. They are trying everything they can to be a better player and sometimes help them 12._____ from injuries. I have to keep learning and expand my knowledge to be able to help players. That process never ends. It's very challenging.

Match the words to describe the good and challenging parts of baseball jobs.

A		B		C	
life-long	player	great	challenges	team	center
baseball	time	cold	luck	trade	camaraderie
little	relationships	job	call	media	players

D. Which Jobs From Part B Would You Recommend to the People Below?

Compare your choices with a partner.

1. Claudio has experience evaluating players, likes to travel, and speaks English. He is also very good at reading people. He has coached pro ball in Italy.

2. Hae-lee enjoys working with children and teens. She has worked as a volunteer in Little League and with some schools.

3. Juan Soto grew up in Colombia and studied English in New York for a year during university. He also has excellent writing and presenting skills.

4. Yuki played in a professional baseball league in Japan. She has a lot of experience as a player and coach, and in analytics. She also knows how to evaluate players.

5. Jean-Pierre loves exercise and fitness. He believes in eating healthy and stretching and has a master's degree in athletic training. JP also has a passion for yoga and meditation.

E. Discussion Questions

Of all the jobs you learned about in this section:

1. Which person do you want to meet the most? Why?
2. What is one question you would ask that person?

Insider Advice: Interpreter

With more non-native speakers of English coming to play in MLB and a lot of players from English-speaking areas seeking to play in Latin America and Asia, the job of interpreter is becoming more important. These jobs exist throughout MLB, KBO, NPB, CPBL, Caribbean Winter Leagues, and international baseball competitions ex. national teams. Do you have the skills needed to work this job?

- Excellent language skills
- Knowledge of specialized baseball vocabulary and slang in both languages you interpret
- Experience in baseball
- Ability to assist foreign players with their daily needs in-season

1. When have you seen an interpreter do their job in baseball-related activities?
2. Why do you think this job is very important in baseball?
3. Suppose an interpreter has strong general language skills but does not know much technical baseball vocabulary. What do you think may

6. Help Wanted: Finding a Job in Baseball

"The Oakland A's are currently seeking…"

A. Pre-Reading Warm-Up
Your dream job?
1. Review the baseball job listing descriptions in exercise C.
2. Rank the jobs in order of the ones you would like to do most to least. Why?
3. Which job do you think you are most qualified for?
   You have the skills to do this job, now!

B. Vocabulary
1. Complete the WORD SCRAMBLE. These words can be found in the reading below.

1. tassis	5. isaetsaonp
2. asttesda	6. ad cho
3. legomind	7. nalaesos
4. lelfexib	8. atiedmtes

C. Read the Partial Job Descriptions
Optional: Try reading aloud with a partner. Take turns reading after a sentence or two.

Search: Baseball Jobs
source: SimplyHired.com

Read these partial baseball job descriptions from the web. Which ones would you click on?

Baseball Operations Intern
Oakland Athletics - Oakland, CA 4.4
The Oakland Athletics are currently seeking individuals passionate about baseball, statistics, and related research for a Baseball Operations Intern position in…
Estimated: $27,000 - $36,000 a year

Twins/ Baseball Beat Reporter

*Star Tribune Media Company LLC - Minneapolis, MN 3.6
The Star Tribune is looking for a beat reporter to cover the Minnesota Twins baseball team. This writer will report from Twins games at home and on the road,…*

Flexible schedule! Baseball Cashiers NEEDED

*Dell Diamond - Round Rock, TX 4.3
We are holding a job fair to kick off our Baseball Season and are looking for all types of new staff from full time to seasonal to help in our food service…*
$10 - $15 an hour

MLB Gameday Compliance Monitor (Seasonal) - Atlanta, Georgia
MLB Data Operations - Atlanta, GA +10 locations
Monitor the storage and handling of baseballs. Strong knowledge of baseball and MLB rules. Ability to effectively communicate to Major League Baseball personnel...
Estimated: $18,000 - $25,000 a year

Baseball Analytics Associate

DETROIT TIGERS, INC. - Detroit, MI 4.1
Assist with statistical modeling of baseball data. Assist with importing, cleaning, and preparing of baseball datasets. Design ad hoc SQL queries.

Estimated: $26,000 - $34,000 a year

Baseball Coach 7th/8th Grade (OMS)

Stillwater Area Public Schools - Stillwater, MN 3.6

7th/8th Grade Boys Baseball Coach. All other Coaching duties as assigned by head baseball coach. To provide an opportunity for the development of the...

Estimated: $28,000 - $39,000 a year

D. Cluster Challenge:
Complete the Collocations Using These Words:
full/flexible/duties/reporter/food

1. She worked _____ time for almost 70 years.
2. He was promoted to the Cavaliers beat _____ in 2003, the year the team drafted Lebron James first overall.
3. _____ service is a tough business.
4. Schultz has taken over coaching _____ –leading practices, running drills, ordering uniforms, organizing trips to games.
5. I do early morning workouts, but eat when I get to work at 10 AM because I have a _____ schedule.

E. Agree or Disagree
Do you agree with the following statements? Discuss with a partner (if possible).

Agree or Disagree

1. There are baseball jobs you can work only during the baseball season.
2. Jobs in analytics seem interesting to me.
3. I have the skills to do at least one of these jobs.
4. I would apply for one of the coaching jobs.

F. Discussion: You Make the Call
1. Which of these jobs do you want to do most, and why?
2. Which of these jobs do you want to do least, and why?
3. Which job do you feel most qualified for, and why?

7. Putting It All Together

A. From what you learned so far in this unit, write about three baseball jobs that interest you. Include the *job title*, job description, and *why you want this job*. Congratulations, you are on your way to a job in baseball!

1. Job title_____ | Skills needed:_____
Description: | Why do you want this job?
_____ | _____
_____ | _____

2. Job title_____ | Skills needed:_____
Description: | Why do you want this job?
_____ | _____
_____ | _____

3. Job title_____ | Skills needed:_____
Description: | Why do you want this job?
_____ | _____
_____ | _____

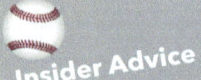

Insider Advice

The clubbie or clubhouse attendant works hard to help the team, ex. they make sure the team has clean uniforms, good clubhouse food, and other requests. At the MLB level, it is customary to tip them with some cash. **Don't forget your *clubbie*!**

What are some other jobs at the ballpark?

B. Role Play: Job Discussion

Walk around and ask classmates about a job they chose to describe. Then write down what they said below.

Ask:

	1	2	3
Name of the person you spoke to			
Which baseball job would you like to do the most?			
What skills do you need?			
Why do you want this job?			
Are you qualified to do this job now? Do you have all the necessary skills and experience?			

8. Reading Spotlight

Pioneering GM signs Trailblazers: *He was fearless ... sellout crowds, flashing lights*

A. Key Vocabulary Review
Here are key terms related to the reading below.
Match the terms (1-9) with the definitions (a-i).

1. ___ personality
2. ___ trailblazer
3. ___ cheerleader
4. ___ ultra-calm
5. ___ modern-era
6. ___ excitement
7. ___ takeaway
8. ___ talent
9. ___ flier

a. a person who encourages other people to do or support something
b. a feeling of eager enthusiasm and interest
c. to do something that could have either good or bad results
d. the present or recent times
e. attractive qualities (such as energy, friendliness, and humor) that make a person interesting or pleasant to be with
f. a main point or key message to be learned or understood from something experienced or observed
g. a special ability that allows someone to do something well
h. a person who makes, does, or discovers something new and makes it acceptable or popular
i. a very quiet and peaceful state or condition

B. Use the Words From A (1-9) to complete the Passage Below

C. Read
Optional: Try reading aloud with a partner. Take turns reading after a sentence or two.

Fred Claire, Los Angeles Dodgers GM (1987-98), signed many players throughout his long tenure as GM. One highlight of that career started when he received a phone call from agent Arn Tellem, who told him about player agent Don Nomura, who was representing a player from Japan, called Hideo Nomo. Claire did not know either of them.

The Dodgers went on to sign Hideo Nomo from Japan in 1995. He retired from playing in NPB to follow his dream of pursuing an MLB career. Also, Mr. Claire and the Dodgers signed Chan-ho Park out of South Korea. These signings opened many doors for players in Japan, South Korea, and, later, Taiwan. Hideo Nomo making the leap from Japan to MLB created a new pipeline of players coming from Asia to MLB, eventually landing other superstars like Ichiro Suzuki to play in the States. This also started a new base of MLB fans from Asia, cheering on their favorite players in MLB.

Claire, GM of the 1988 World Series Champions, shared his insightful thoughts on these signings and more in a conversation with Philip Riccobono.

• *Hideo Nomo is a 1. _____ in MLB during the 2. _____. By signing him did you hope to open the door for other Japanese-born players to make the jump to MLB or was it just a 3. _____, since it was at first a minor league signing?*

From the very beginning, I saw the signing of Hideo as a great opportunity for the Dodgers and for Hideo himself. Bringing in a player from Japan with the potential for that player's success carried both potential and excitement. And once we had reports on Hideo's makeup and ability, the goal became very clear to sign Hideo if at all possible. We had talked to several scouts who had seen Hideo and former players who had faced him in Japan. This clearly was a special player.

• *Were you surprised that player agent, Don Nomura, was able to orchestrate Nomo's retirement and you'd have a chance to sign him?*

I found Don to be the perfect person to represent Hideo in that Don understood players, had a great personal history in the game, and was both smart and competitive. Don clearly wasn't afraid of challenging a longstanding system to provide the best representation for Hideo and other players. He knew what it was like to be a player and face challenges and had a good sense of business.

• *Although Hideo was not the first Japanese-born player in MLB, Nomo had a lot of weight on his shoulders; at first, many in Japan did not approve of his move to the States. He had a lot to prove. Did you ever discuss this with him? If so, could you elaborate?*

Once meeting Hideo, there was no question in my mind but that he understood the challenge that he faced and realized his performance would have a major impact on both baseball in Japan and on other players from Japan. In my mind, Hideo was very media-savvy because he understood what it was like to be a featured player in Japan and the focus that would be on him on a daily basis.

• *Later, you also signed Chan-ho Park, who was the first South Korean to play in MLB. Again, did you hope to open up South Korea baseball to MLB?*

Chan-ho Park, like Hideo, had both great 4. _____ with great character and 5. _____. The game excitement was there with the opportunity to sign Chan-ho because the Dodgers always had placed an emphasis on international talent and this was opening on a new part of the baseball world.

Fred Claire (L) with Hideo Nomo (C)

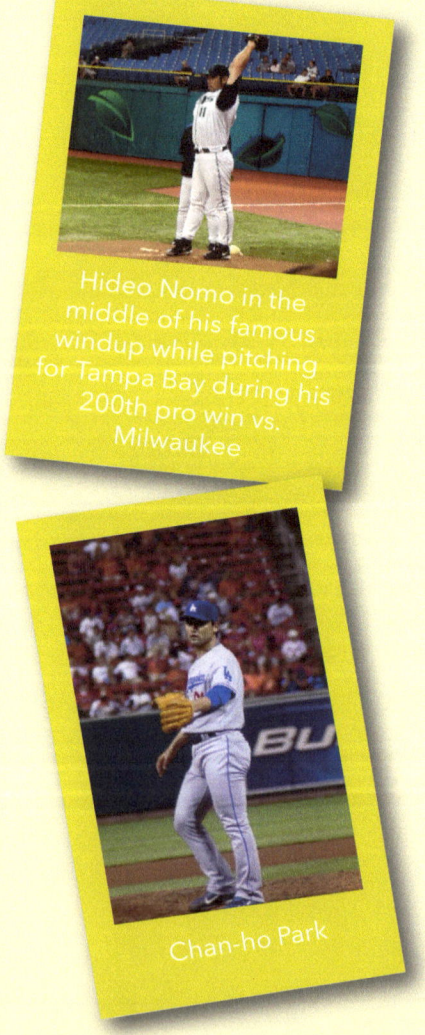

Hideo Nomo in the middle of his famous windup while pitching for Tampa Bay during his 200th pro win vs. Milwaukee

Chan-ho Park

• How do you feel about the success of some Japanese and Korean players over the last three decades in MLB? This happened in part [because of] your work.

I'm proud to have had a role in signing both Hideo and Chan-ho but this was possible due to the great vision and leadership of the O'Malley family and the ultimate success of the players was a credit to the tremendous coaching and leadership of the people in our player development department.

• Nomo had a special relationship with Tommy Lasorda, as evident in a YouTube video entitled "Tommy Lasorda Teaches Hideo Nomo I Bleed Dodger Blue!" In this video, the manager taught Nomo to say, "I bleed Dodger Blue." As someone who's been working inside Japanese baseball for over a decade, I'm pretty sure Nomo did not experience a relationship like that with a manager before. Has that ever been expressed by Nomo to you? Could you comment on that?

Tommy was the perfect manager for Hideo in every way. His outgoing personality made Hideo feel welcome and wanted. I'm sure it was totally different from what Hideo had experienced in Japan and it had to be a welcoming and refreshing change. Tommy was never a critic of Hideo and always a 6. _____. Tommy quickly saw the impact that Hideo could make on our team.

• From soup to nuts, what's your biggest 7. _____ from your experience during Nomo-mania?

Sellout crowds, flashing lights from cameras to capture the
8. _____, a major following by the Japanese media and the 9. _____ personality of a polished professional who knew the stage was set for him and he was going to take advantage of the opportunity. He was fearless!

D. Everyday English: Idioms

> **EVERYDAY ENGLISH IDIOMS:** *From Soup to Nuts*
>
> **Idioms** are word combinations that have a different figurative meaning than the literal **meanings** of each word or phrase. They can be confusing for kids or people learning English, as they don't mean what they say, ex. *break a leg*, *kick the bucket*, *down the road*.
>
> *From soup to nuts* is a common idiom in Everyday English. You might think that someone is talking about food, but it means *from the beginning to end* or *from start to finish*. The phrase comes from the serving of a full course meal, which typically began with some type of soup and ended with a dessert containing nuts.
> *Source: 7ESL.com*
>
> 1. What are some other idioms you know?
> 2. Share one idiom you know with a partner and discuss its meaning.

E. Are the Sentences True (T) or False (F)? If False (F), Correct the Sentence.

True or False

1. The Dodgers took a flier on Nomo and did not know much about the player.
2. Don Nomura had all the tools as an agent to sign Hideo Nomo.
3. Claire takes all the credit for Nomo and Park's success.
4. Nomo's managers in Japan probably had a very different style compared to Tommy Lasorda.
5. Nomo-mania represented something extraordinary and exciting in Dodger history.

F. **Talk TIME**

1. How many years did Fred Claire work as the Dodgers' GM?
2. Do many general managers have a chance to work as a GM for that long with one club in MLB today? Why or why not?
3. Who are some players from Asia who have been successful or popular in MLB? What do you like about them?
4. Are the managers and coaches you have worked with been very strict or more relaxed? Which style do you prefer, and why?
5. Which other parts of Asia did the Dodgers sign players?

UNIT 8
Baseballisms: A Very Unique, Complex Language

Topics: Understanding Baseball Talk, Crossword challenge, Translation, Vocabulary study—what do you know, Podcasts, Red ass, International expert, Take me out to the ball game…

1. Batter Up! Vocabulary

A. Here Are Some Terms Related to Unique Baseball Talk

Match the terms (1-11) with the definitions (a-k).

1. ___ cryptic
2. ___ insular
3. ___ language
4. ___ curse words
5. ___ off-putting
6. ___ fuck, fuckin'
7. ___ metaphors
8. ___ confusing
9. ___ tone
10. ___ ass
11. ___ slang

a) the part of the body above the legs that is used for sitting
b) difficult to understand
c) having or seeming to have a hidden meaning
d) offensive words that people say when they are angry or want to emphasize something
e) often associated with anger; an insult and considered very offensive. However, it may not represent anger or negativity when used as a modifier, expressively accentuating a point
f) separated from other people or cultures
g) a word or phrase for one thing that is used to refer to another thing in order to show or suggest that they are similar
h) not pleasing or likable; causing you to dislike someone or something
i) a quality, feeling, or attitude expressed by the words that someone uses in speaking or writing
j) words that are not considered part of the standard vocabulary of a language and that are used very informally in speech, especially by a particular group of people
k) the system of words or signs that people use to express thoughts and feelings to each other

B. Use the Words From Above (1-11) to Complete the Passage Below

Understanding Baseball Talk

Philip Riccobono's research in English for Baseball Purposes aims to improve communication in baseball where English is the common 1._____ . Some of Baseball English is very 2._____ and not accessible to the public. It might seem 3._____ as it consists of unique vocabulary used only in the sport (*fungo, Mendoza line*). Baseball includes words that have more than one meaning within the sport ex. *ball, run, hit, pick*. The sport includes plenty of 4._____ (*cheese, heat, swinging a wet newspaper, dotting a gnat's* 5._____ *, knocking the crap outta the ball, that guy just tittied that ball*) and some 6._____

that is very 7._____ (8._____, shit, *motherfucker–considered highly offensive). So, paying close attention to the spoken tone of some words, particularly these 9._____ can help you understand the importance of a situation compared to just reading them. The 10._____ of a person's voice while using off-putting words will help you understand whether or not they are angry. To make baseball even more difficult, it includes terms with meanings used outside of the sport (*slider*, *bag*, *steal*). Therefore, Baseball English may seem 11._____ and confusing to many, including those whose first language is English.

However, Baseball English can unite a team of players from around the world whose first language is other than English and improve their success. In this unit, you will learn some very unfamiliar vocabulary that makes Baseball English so unique.

C. Agree or Disagree

Do you agree with the following statements? Discuss with others. *Agree or Disagree*

1. Learning Baseball English is not necessary for me.
2. Baseball uses words that have more thanone meaning.
3. I can understand someone without paying attention to the tone of their voice.
4. Off-putting curse words should not be used in baseball.

D. Discussion Questions
1. How can learning Baseball English help you?
2. What's most difficult thing about Baseball English?
3. What do you like most about Baseball English?
4. What are some words in baseball English that have more than one meaning in the sport, ex. run, ball?
5. What is some baseball slang you know, in English and in your first language? slang you know, in English and in your first language?

Did You Know?
Interpreter: Time's a Tickin'

In a study on the importance of learning Baseball English, one former MLB employee gave their opinion on the need for Baseball English on the field in North America. They said, "An interpreter may only come out for a limited amount of time. The pitching coach speaks English, the catcher speaks Spanish, and the first baseman speaks Korean; you have one interpreter out there. There's no way that that's [a message or point] getting communicated in 30 seconds." Unfortunately, in some cases, interpreters have been considered *outsiders* with little or no baseball experience, perhaps making it more challenging to communicate unfamiliar baseball words and phrases.

1. In this case, what is the biggest challenge for the interpreter?
2. If you were an interpreter, how would you prepare to do your best?
3. In your opinion, what kind of job and life experience does a baseball interpreter need to have?

2. Crossword Challenge

As mentioned in the above reading, baseball vocabulary or jargon consists of slang and metaphors that are considered cryptic and confusing. This crossword puzzle includes unique Baseball English.

A.

Baseballisms
Complete the crossword puzzle below

bandbox   knockdown   dotting a gnat's ass   red ass   brushback   tired act   false hustle
jam   cannon   shove   wear it   cheese

Across
3. cheering on your teammates and encouraging them after taking a hit and also can be a command for those who are scared to take
8. when the pitch is thrown near the batter's hands
10. when a pitcher shows pinpoint command
11. a small ballpark in which it is easy to hit home runs
12. an extremely strong arm

Down
1. fastball
2. a player pretends to be real angry at a player on another team, which can lead to a fight
4. someone is very angry and intense towards something
5. A high-and-tight pitch designed to keep the batter from crowding the plate
6. appearing to work hard when in reality it is not productive
7. to pitch very well
9. any pitch that sends a hitter into the dirt

B. Keywords in context (KWIC) challenge:

Complete the sentence using these terms.
false hustle/red ass/wear it/swinging a wet newspaper/tired act

1. He said, after striking out with a runner on in the ninth inning of a 14-12 loss, that it felt like he was _____ and that his bat speed was "completely gone" because of the weakening state of the left wrist he fractured.
2. It's a _____ . He's just trying to get in his head.
3. Eyewash is baseball slang for _____ or working hard for the appearance of working hard.
4. But captain _____ Brian McCann wasn't satisfied with just hollering like he did with Jose Fernandez. This time, he met Gomez halfway up the third baseline, blocking his path to the plate.
5. There is no excuse for ducking out of the way of an inside off-speed pitch. As long as you _____ properly, it's not going to hurt. It's a free base, and you'll smile down the line.

3. Role Play: Team Interpreter

A. Imagine you work as the team interpreter. Part of your job includes interpreting *baseballisms*.

Interpret Baseballisms from English to your language.

English ➡ Your first language or another language

1. The catcher tells the pitcher: "Show me the **cheese**!"
   _____
   _____

2. A manager says to a player: "Stop the **false hustle**!"
   _____
   _____

3. The pitching coach says: "Throw a **knockdown** pitch."
   _____
   _____

4. A player on their comments on their hitting performance: "I'm swinging a **wet newspaper**."
   _____
   _____

B. Take Turns Interpreting the Above Statements to a Partner in Their First Language

C. Go for It

*Replace the bold words (A. page 95) with other slang terms from the crossword puzzle (page 94) or other baseball terms you know, ex. Show me the **slider**.*

Practice saying those phrases.

a. Show me the _____.
b. Throw a _____ pitch.
c. They've got a _____ for an arm.

University baseball team members in South Korea contribute to the vocabulary study.

Dr. Riccobono with participants of this study at a high school in Chiba, Japan.

4. Research in Baseball Vocabulary:

What Words Do You Know?

Dr. Philip Riccobono conducted a study of 261 baseball specialists—players, coaches, umpires, administrators, scouts—whose first language was other than English, on their knowledge of frequently used core-user* spoken baseball vocabulary. The results of a listening exam indicated that participants' knowledge of single words (56%) was significantly greater than multiple word baseball terms (34%). This is understandable, as comprehension of multiple-word terms (*opposite field, home run, front side closure-see the appendix for more of these phrases*) requires more memory. This study suggests that there is room for improvement in knowledge of baseball vocabulary for specialists whose first language is other than English, especially for multiple-word terms.

*core-user: baseball players, coaches, umpires, scouts, team personnel, etc.

Single-word Knowledge Test Results

1. field*: 72%
2. player*: 94%
3. base*: 94%
4. movement*: 72%
5. balance*: 59%
6. cage*: 42%
7. spin*: 77%
8. bag*: 62%
9. attaboy: 37%
10. bullpen: 66%
11. bunt: 93%
12. changeup: 94%
13. coach: 91%
14. curveball: 55%
15. fastball: 92%
16. fungo: 32%
17. oppo: 70%
18. routine: 89%
19. scoreboard: 85%
20. slump: 90%

*Frequently used words in English from a commonly used wordlist called General Service List (GSL). This list is recommended for learning English vocabulary and is available for free on the Internet.

A. Listen Up!

What do you know?

Have someone read you the words from the blue box on the previous page. Write down the words you know in the box below and also write the words you do not know. It's important to hear the words because in most cases, for baseball jobs such as player, coach, or umpire, you'll speak about baseball rather than write about it.

High school baseball club student managers completing the vocabulary listening exam on their smartphones. Nagoya, Japan.

Words I know	Words I need to learn

B. Discussion Questions

1. Based on the results of the study from page 96:
    a. Which three words do these baseball specialists need to learn the most?
    b. Which three terms do these baseball specialists seem most familiar with?

2. How do you think baseball specialists whose language is other than English can improve their knowledge of spoken baseball vocabulary used by players, coaches, umpires, etc.?

3. In languages other than English, some baseball vocabulary terms from this study are used (Japanese, Korean, Spanish).
    a. Which of the terms from this study are used in baseball language from your country?
    b. Which of the terms are not used in your first language and what is the translation from English to your language?

5. Baseballism Video: Red Ass

A. Warm-Up

1. Have you ever tried to stop a fight or an argument from happening? If yes, can you describe what happened?

B. Reading Body Language
Understanding body language can help you know what someone is saying. Match the pictures (A-B) with the phrase (1-2).
1. "It's cool. It's cool."
2. "I like that."

A.

B.

C. Vocabulary
These words and phrases are used in the video that you will watch and listen to. Match the opposites.
1. little bit   2. little life   3. cool   4. break it up
a. allow conflict   b. much   c. emotionless   d. angry

Did You Know?

Podcasts are a good way to learn English. You will hear the hosts and the people they interview speak naturally. This helps build your vocabulary and listening skills. Japan Baseball Weekly (JBW) covers all 12 NPB teams. The hosts, John E. Gibson and Jim Allen, live in the Tokyo area and have reported on baseball in Japan for decades.

Some podcast listeners, whose first language is not English, find value in listening to the show. "One Japanese listener we had a couple of years back said she was able to follow because of the show information on the iTunes app and the fact that we talk about the topics to be discussed each week in the show opening," said Gibson, a Japanese baseball journalist who has been based in Japan since the 1990s. Gibson, who started the podcast in 2010, recalls how one Japanese listener was impressed with the hosts' knowledge of the Japanese game. The listener said it was even "better than mine." That was strange to him because Gibson and Allen are non-native speakers of Japanese.

To improve your English and learn from seasoned NPB media, try listening to this podcast. Also, there are many other baseball-related podcasts in English, discussing MLB, KBO, other international baseball leagues and teams. For example Trevor Raichura hosts H-TEN, covering the Hanshin Tigers.

1. Do you listen to baseball podcasts in English?
2. Check the Internet. What are three popular baseball podcasts in English? Which of these three podcasts would you listen to first, and why?

You can learn more about baseball in Japan by following the hosts of JBW:
John Gibson's Twitter: @JBWPodcast – Jim Allen's weekly newsletter: www.jballen.com, Twitter @jballallen

D. Watch and Listen-In

*Now, let's listen in as players and the manager get **fired up** during a **heated** exchange with their opponents.*

Note: The dialogue below begins at 0:31, but watch from the beginning to understand the situation.

Please go to www.sportsEnglish.org/media (video 14)

1. Complete the table below.

Red Ass Dialogue

Circle one	Fill in the blanks	Notes — Which words or phrases do you need to learn?
Player or Manager	"We're just trying to _____ . We're just trying to break it up, man. We're just trying to break it up, man. _____."	
Player or Manager	"Alright. I like to see a little life once in a while. You guys got a little bit of _____ in ya, _____ . Little bit of red ass in us."	

2. Practice reading the dialogue with a partner if possible.

E. Discussion Questions

1. Do you agree with getting very excited and showing emotion in baseball and other sports? Why?
2. Have you ever had, or experienced someone else having, "red ass" during a baseball game or practice? If so, explain what happened.
3. After watching this video, who do you think is wrong here: the catcher or the batter? Why?

> **CONVERSATION STRATEGY SPOTLIGHT**
> ***BREAK IT UP*** • In the video, the player, Doc Brooks, said, "We're just trying to **break it up**" during that heated moment. What were the players trying to **break up**?

F. Role Play: Break It Up!

As we saw in the video, "break it up" was said to stop an argument. "Break it up" can also be used for a physical fight. Practice the argument from the Red Ass video between the players. At least one person needs to join in, trying to stop the argument by saying "break it up." Use emotion to make the argument seem real. Think of new arguments and write them below.

Example
Argument topic: I'm a better pitcher than you.
A: I can throw much faster than you. My fastball velo is 94MPH.
B: Well, I can throw a much better slider than you.
A: No, you can't!
B: Yes, I can!
C: Alright. *Break it up! Break it up!*

Try It: You "Break It Up!"

Write a dialogue with an argument and then use "break it up" to stop the fight.
A: _____
B: _____
A: _____
B: _____
C: _____

Insider Advice
ASAP

One of the jobs of a team interpreter is to help the player with off-field tasks such as ordering batting gloves. Some years ago, an American baseball player in Japan asked his interpreter to order batting gloves. After a few weeks, the player asked for the batting gloves. The interpreter forgot to put in the order and apologized. He said he would do it right away. The player told him, "Hurry up, I want the gloves ASAP!"

Well, the gloves arrived a few weeks later with "ASAP" written on them. This was a misunderstanding, as the interpreter thought the player wanted the gloves to say "ASAP" on them because he stressed "ASAP" when instructing the interpreter to hurry up and get him the batting gloves. **The moral of the story is to try to understand even the smallest details of what your player said.**

1. What could the interpreter have done differently to avoid ordering gloves that said "ASAP"?

2. As we just learned, interpreters have a lot of responsibility in communicating the correct message. When are some other times that the interpreter could make mistakes communicating if not careful?

6. Reading Spotlight: Expert Opinion

"Saw four umpires with interpreters and four different languages try and come to an agreement"

Warm-Up
Who do you think of as a baseball expert in your country? Why are they an expert?

A. Vocabulary
Here are some terms related to the reading below.
Match the terms (1-6) with the definitions (a-f).

1. competition
2. common
3. expert
4. international
5. native
6. technical vocabulary

a. occurring frequently
b. involving two or more countries
c. belonging to a person since birth or childhood
d. trying to win something
e. terms used in a specific field
f. having a special knowledge

"A Slow Tennis Match"

As mentioned earlier in this unit, insider Baseball English is often confusing or tricky, filled with slang and metaphors that may seem foreign even to native English speakers. Therefore, the role of interpreters during international baseball competition is very important. They must have great knowledge and practice of not only general English but also technical baseball vocabulary and slang. This is because English is the common language used during international competition.

While working with USA Baseball, Steve Cohen witnessed how perhaps a lack of communication led to an approximately 25-minute game delay in international competition (USA versus Cuba). Cohen, who has worked for over 40 years in baseball as a coach, MLB international scout, and USA Baseball director, feels that learning Baseball English "is needed for international competition." During an argument on the field, Cohen "saw four umpires with interpreters and four different languages try and come to an agreement on a call and it was like watching a slow tennis match progress." This kind of situation will slow the game and possibly create confusion. Knowledge of Baseball English by all those involved in the game during international competition will perhaps improve this situation, especially among coaches, managers, and umpires.

Steve Cohen, international baseball expert

101

B. Are the Sentences True (T) or False (F)? If False (F), Correct the Sentence.

True or False

1. Cohen thought the communication went well between players, coaches, and umpires on the field at the Olympic event discussed in this reading.
2. Interpreters need to know Baseball English.
3. The role of the interpreter in international baseball competition is not that important.
4. Cohen compared the on-field discussion between interpreters, umpires, and coaches to a fast-paced ice hockey game.
5. Normally, during international competition, players and coaches communicate with umpires in English.
6. It's a good idea for all involved in international baseball competition to understand Baseball English.

C. Discussion Questions

1. Do you agree with Cohen's opinion that players, coaches, umpires, and interpreters need to learn Baseball English for international competition, ex. Olympics, World Baseball Classic, SEA Games, etc.? Why or why not?

2. What recommendations do you have for improving communication between players, coaches, and umpires during international competition?

Did You Know?
Baseball Trivia

Many fans enjoy **baseball trivia** about history, players, and other topics related to the sport. Learning baseball trivia allows you to use important language skills: reading, writing, speaking, listening, vocabulary, pronunciation. For example, when viewing trivia questions online, you will *read* them. When *writing* new challenging trivia questions to ask your baseball fan friends, you may research players' awards and impressive statistics. Then you may use your speaking and listening *skills* in a baseball trivia meeting or competition, which you may do online with friends from all over the world. So, find some baseball trivia questions or write them yourself and ask others if they know the answers. You may even have a few laughs during a friendly competition while learning new vocabulary and working on pronunciation about English and baseball trivia!

University English professors in Japan and South Korea compete virtually during their monthly Baseball Trivia Night.

Discussion
1. Have you ever participated in baseball trivia?
2.
a. Search the Internet for a baseball trivia question about your favorite player, team, or baseball-related topic.
Write the question here:

_____
_____

b. Ask others the question you wrote. Did they give you the correct answer? Do you think it was an easy or difficult question? Why or why not?

Some Baseball Trivia Links
mlb.com/trivia
worldhistoryproject.org/quizzes/baseball

BONUS ACTIVITY
Baseball History & Culture: *Take Me Out to the Ball Game*

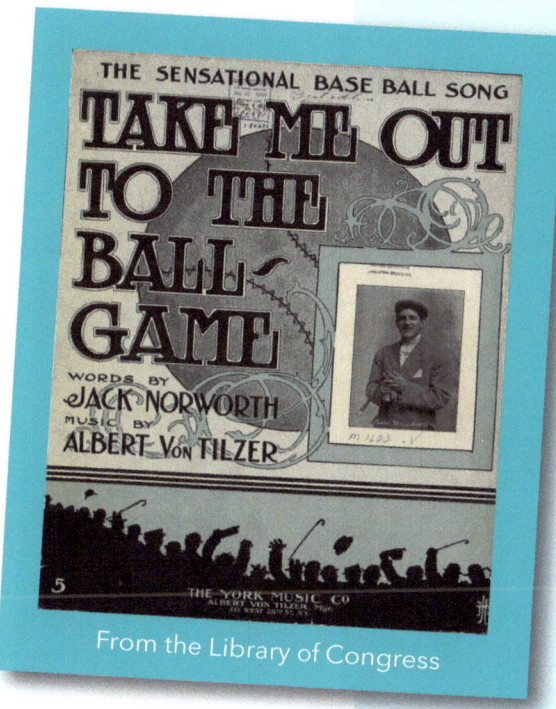
From the Library of Congress

On May 2, 1908, "Take Me Out to the Ball Game" was published. It was composed by Albert von Tilzer with words written by Jack Norworth. The song has become the official anthem of North American baseball, although its authors had never attended a ball game before writing the song. The original version of the song, which you will hear (in exercise C), was sung by Edward Meeker in 1908 and is one of the first recordings of the song.

The song's chorus is traditionally sung during the middle of the seventh inning of a baseball game. Fans are generally encouraged to sing along, and at most ballparks, the words "home team" are replaced with the home team's name.

A. Warm-Up
1. Did you know that the song is not about baseball?
2. What are some popular foods and drinks at North American ball games?

B. Vocabulary
Match the terms that have similar meanings.
1. peanut   2. root   3. crowd   4. shame   5. home team

a. playing on its own field   b. people   c. goober   d. cheer on   e. bad luck

C. Listen to part of the original song

complete the gap-filling exercise below using the terms from above (1-5).
*You may use one of the terms more than once.
Go to: www.sportsEnglish.org/media (audio 1)

> **Take Me Out to the Ball Game**
>
> Take me out to the ball game, Take me out with the_____ ;
> Buy me some_____ and Cracker Jack, I don't care if I never get
> back. Let me _____ , _____ , _____ for the
> home team, If they don't win, it's a _____ . For it's one, two,
> three strikes, you're out, At the old _____ game.

Don't forget to replace "home team" with the name of your favorite team.

D. Sing!

Sing the lyrics to **Take Me Out to the Ball Game** *in a group or alone.*
Listen to this version of the song heard at many North American ballparks
(with no lyrics) on a traditional organ.
Go to: www.sportsEnglish.org/media (audio 2)

E. Discussion Questions

1. Does your country have a special tradition during the middle of the seventh inning?
2. What are some fan traditions during ball games in your country—foods, drinks, songs, chants, etc.? Which are your favorites, and why?

To request the Answer Key and A-Z Words and Phrases list
go to: www.sportsEnglish.org/request

About the author

Philip S. Riccobono is a lecturer of English at Himeji Dokkyo University and a professional baseball scout. He is the author of *Triangulating Diamond Talk: Identifying Technical Spoken Vocabulary in English For Baseball Purposes*. His work has appeared in such publications as *Journal of English for Specific Purposes at Tertiary Level* and *STEM Journal*. Originally from the United States, he lives in Kobe, Japan with his wife, Keiko, and sons, Tomoki and Shoei. For additional information on Baseball and Sports English, go to www.sportsEnglish.org.

Philip and Doala at Vantelin Dome Nagoya

www.ingramcontent.com/pod-product-compliance
Lightning Source LLC
Chambersburg PA
CBHW041536220426
43663CB00002B/54